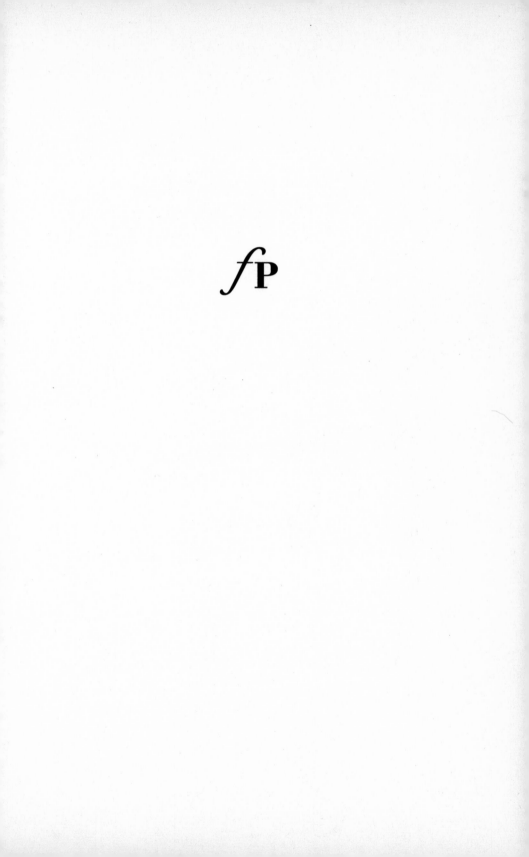

THEATER GEEK

THE REAL LIFE DRAMA OF A SUMMER AT STAGEDOOR MANOR, THE FAMOUS PERFORMING ARTS CAMP

Mickey Rapkin

Free Press

New York   London   Toronto   Sydney

FREE PRESS

A Division of Simon & Schuster, Inc.
1230 Avenue of the Americas
New York, NY 10020

First Free Press hardcover edition June 2010

FREE PRESS and colophon are trademarks of Simon & Schuster, Inc.

For information about special discounts for bulk purchases, please contact Simon & Schuster Special Sales at 1-866-506-1949 or business@simonandschuster.com.

The Simon & Schuster Speakers Bureau can bring authors to your live event. For more information or to book an event contact the Simon & Schuster Speakers Bureau at 1-866-248-3049 or visit our website at www.simonspeakers.com.

DESIGNED BY DANIEL LAGIN

Manufactured in the United States of America

10   9   8   7   6   5   4   3   2

Library of Congress Cataloging-in-Publication Data

Rapkin, Mickey.
Theater geek : the real life drama of a summer at Stagedoor Manor, the famous perorming arts camp / Mickey Rapkin.
p.   cm.
1. Stagedoor Manor (Loch Sheldrake, N.Y.) 2. Acting—Study and teaching—New York (State)—Loch Sheldrake. 3. Teenage actors—New York (State)—Loch Sheldrake. I. Title.
PN 2078.N43.R38 2010
792.02'8071174735—dc22   2009048797

ISBN 978-1-4391-4576-0
ISBN 978-1-4391-5439-7 (ebook)

To Julio

Contents

God sets the lonely in families.

—PSALM 68:6

This season I got my first chance to appear on Broadway and experience what the theater is really all about: Arguing.

—MADONNA, AT THE 1998 TONY AWARDS

THEATER GEEK

Prologue

I SHOULD PROBABLY START WITH A CONFESSION: IN 1994, seated in the audience of the Imperial Theatre on West 45th Street in Manhattan, I cried during the overture to *Les Misérables*. I was sixteen years old, and I was weeping before the curtain even went up. It wasn't sentimentality or a passion for the theater that grabbed me (though I'm a victim of both). It was something purely vicarious. I couldn't get over the idea that an actor was backstage in costume, preparing to go on awash in that awesome sea of pre-show adrenaline. I was jealous, plain and simple. From my seat on the other side (the wrong side?) of the curtain, I imagined the raw anticipation, the all-for-one camaraderie, the happy thrill those lucky few actors must have felt to do what they loved eight times a week. It was too much for my nerves to handle, and they literally flooded.

There's this phrase—*theater geek*—that describes a longing I've had since I was young. As far as I can tell, this particular term didn't appear in print until a 1995 *Washington Times* tribute to Broadway veteran George Abbott, who died that year (at age one hundred and seven!). But it was certainly in colloquial usage before then. Because that's what kids like me were. Theater geeks. Performances, and performers, meant the world to me then, and I worshipped the people who could do professionally what I could only attempt in my earnest high school productions on suburban Long Island. I had a great many friends as a teenager, but almost none I could talk to about crying at *Les Misérables*. In late 1994 I remember taking the train to Manhattan, with some urgency, for a weekend matinee of Stephen Sondheim's *Passion*. Why the rush? The closing notice was posted sooner than expected and I felt like I should really see the show. You know, so I could be *conversant* about it. Conversant with whom? Lord knows. Today, I have only a vague memory of that musical's plot. But I can still recall exactly how it felt sitting in the audience that afternoon when actress Marin Mazzie put a little extra zing on the end of the lyric, "Imagine that, a whole forty days. Well, *forty matinees.*" She was winking at the audience, acknowledging the untimely death the show faced. And we all laughed. *Forty matinees!* The silly general public had once again failed to recognize Sondheim's genius, but we true fans knew better. Truth be told, I didn't love *Passion,* but I certainly loved being in on the joke.

As a teenager, I fantasized about getting a part-time job as a Broadway usher. "You have to join the union," an elderly woman told me at a matinee of *Blood Brothers,* a musical I saw four times in six months. (No wonder it held such sway over me; it's a tearjerker about two boys who never felt comfortable in their own skin.) The old lady leaned in and advised me against pursuing work as an usher. "The money isn't good," she whispered. But I wouldn't have cared. In those years, I never felt alive anywhere except in those cramped, worn-in Broadway seats.

It's telling that I dreamt of being an usher, and not of a life onstage. It simply did not occur to me that I could make a career of the high school drama club, of those Saturday afternoon rehearsals. Part of the reason I quit acting is that I never found a like-minded community to draw from. Looking back, perhaps I wish I'd had a teacher tell me that something more was possible. That, as Sondheim wrote, I could "make a hat where there never was a hat."

Recently a good friend of mine told me about a place I would have loved as a sixteen-year-old tacking up Playbills on his bedroom wall. A place where being a theater geek was not some vague embarrassment about an interest in something supposedly uncool. As it turns out, a whole movement of young theater geeks has been convening in, of all places, the Catskills for decades.

They gather at Stagedoor Manor, a bucolic summer camp where children put up thirteen full-scale productions every three weeks. Stagedoor Manor, my friend explained, is a place where talent scouts come armed with business cards—tiny pieces of paper that can change a kid's life. A place where the love of theater is so pure the kids refuse to employ microphones—even in musicals. (As David Mamet once said, if you're an actor and can't make yourself heard in a thousand-seat theater, you're doing something wrong.) A place where the popular campers are popular *because* of their talent, not despite it. Since 1975, the philosophy at Stagedoor has always been that it's a place for kids to be who they need to be in a safe, nonjudgmental environment. It's an oasis where a six-foot-four, eighteen-year-old boy and a ten-year-old girl walk side by side, talking about the tap class they just took together. Not surprisingly, Stagedoor Manor was one of the first places where a gay kid from the Midwest (or Midtown) could be an out homosexual. But you could replace the word *gay* with *awkward, self-conscious, green, blue,* or *purple.* The camp provides a haven for any child with a love of the arts who, for whatever reason, feels *other than.*

"As my father used to say, 'Put it this way: you don't need to bring a mitt,'" the actor (and former Stagedoor Manor camper) Zach Braff tells me. "And he was right. But at Stagedoor there was constant hugging and snuggling and affirmation. In the world I was used to, there was none of that. It was culture shock to go back to the public school system."

Thirteen musicals? Talent scouts? I had to see this place for myself. And so, at age thirty-one, I packed a bag and went to theater camp.

———

Stagedoor Manor is nestled on twelve acres in the scenic Catskill Mountains. Once the playground of wealthy Jews (as lovingly depicted in *Dirty Dancing*), these rolling hills have since fallen on hard times, fighting a losing tourist-trap battle against low-cost airfare abroad and the thrill of Atlantic City nickel slots. In the sleepy town of Loch Sheldrake, minutes from camp, the local bar anchors a strip of mostly deserted storefronts, including a movie theater that's still advertising 2006's *Superman Returns*.

But then there's that sign. In theatrical cursive lettering, it reads: Stagedoor Manor.

The camp sits half a mile off Route 52, on the site of the old Karmel Hotel, a once-popular resort that featured an indoor pool, tennis courts, and a nightclub, among other amenities. The Karmel ultimately went into foreclosure, sitting vacant until a builder from New Rochelle, New York, named Carl Samuelson saw the potential beneath the leaky roofs, and installed a theater camp there in 1977.

Not much has changed since, not on the surface, anyway. There are seven performance venues at Stagedoor Manor, eight if you count the front lawn (also known as the Garden Theater). But most of the action takes place inside the main building. Step through the front doors and into the wood-paneled lobby, where industrial-strength carpet contends with the hyperactive feet of three hundred campers. Kids rush past to the right, ducking into the dining room, where they'll eat plates of pizza and chicken fingers beneath large

The Karmel Hotel, the once-popular Catskill Mountains resort property where Carl and Elsie Samuelson would install a theater camp. Having toured several potential locations, Carl chose the twelve-acre Karmel because it had room for theaters.

paintings—replicas of Playbills from shows like *Phantom of the Opera* and *Miss Saigon*. Walk left instead, past a couple of kids playing Ping-Pong and a young girl sight-reading selections from *Wicked* on a piano, and enter the costume shop, one of the few locations on the grounds with air-conditioning.

Thirty years ago, the costume shop was a modest one-room operation with garbage bags full of clothing piled high to the ceiling. These days, it's a twisty cavern of seven spaces stuffed to the gills, yet meticulously organized. Period dress is sorted by decade. There are separate closets for fur coats, for wedding gowns, for military dress. Some of these materials were purchased when shows were produced here for the first time (for example, 1920s bob wigs for a 2008 production of *The Producers*). Other items have been donated. In one closet, there are original costumes from Broadway's *A Chorus Line* hanging next to a $10,000 corset from the national tour of *Spamalot*. It's an eight-year-old's dream dress-up closet. Todd Roberts, the head of the costume shop, says that in the off-season months, when Stagedoor Manor is dark, local townspeople have been known to clip the lock on the door. "They break in to steal Halloween costumes," he says.

Since its inception in the 1970s, the camp's program has been more or less the same. Over the course of each three-week session, children from ages ten to eighteen will mount thirteen full-scale productions, leading some in the theater community to describe Stagedoor as summer stock for kids. The analogy fits. (In 2006, the minimum age for campers was upped from eight to ten. The artistic program was simply too demanding for kids who until recently couldn't read.)

There's magic in this place. Stand in the center of Stagedoor Manor and on any given day one might hear Sondheim pouring out of one rehearsal space, *Annie* from another, *Guys & Dolls* from a third, Shakespearean couplets from yet a fourth.

But no single day at Stagedoor is more intoxicating than the first. Cars full of eager campers (and their anxious parents) drive up to the main entrance, where staff members greet them with applause. Inside the lobby, the artistic staff waits—in costume. Campers flit about with their friends, discussing room assignments but mostly just hugging each other. At the piano, the camp's music directors lead these kids in impromptu sing-alongs of *Avenue Q, Chicago, Rent, Legally Blonde: The Musical,* and even lesser-known works such as *Side Show* (a musical about conjoined twins). For the first time, I understand what the film director Todd Graff meant when he described Stagedoor Manor as Oz: come to Stagedoor and for the first time your world is in color. This is why the staff often greet returning campers with the phrase: "Welcome home."

Passing through those doors, I felt like *Fame* director Alan Parker when he first entered the lunchroom at The High School of Performing Arts. "I could feel the energy and excitement," Parker told the *New*

York Times in 1980. "It was like a microcosm of New York City. In the lunchroom, one kid was eating salad on his lap and reading *Hamlet*. Another was playing the cello. All had a common dream." I half expected Debbie Allen to walk into Stagedoor's cafeteria to declare: "Fame costs. And right here is where you start paying. In sweat."

In many ways Stagedoor Manor is like what is now known as La-Guardia, the school that inspired *Fame*; it's a summer camp but also an elite training ground for some of our nation's most talented young artists. And you will recognize the names of many of Stagedoor alumni. One starred as Sally Bowles in a 1995 camp production of *Cabaret*, which lives on in lore for several reasons. If you happened to be in the audience that night, you would have seen Sally Bowles standing center stage, outfitted in a short red-and-black dress with fringe. The song is "Don't Tell Mama," and she and a dozen Kit Kat Klub girls (each armed with her own chair) dance in unison. Until, that is, the girl to Sally Bowles's left stands up on her chair, loses her balance in mid-song, and wipes out completely, dragging a second girl down to the floor with her.

Natalie Portman played Sally Bowles that night, and a video of the production survives. Watch as Natalie registers the commotion but never breaks character. She doesn't check to see whether the fallen girl is injured, or whether she's in need of assistance. And why should she? When you're a teenage actress starring as a Nazi-era stripper, what choice do you have but to keep on singing? As the emcee says in *Cabaret*, "So, life is disappointing. Forget it!"

Natalie attended Stagedoor Manor for three summers, even while she was working in Hollywood, starring in movies like Luc Besson's *The Professional*. "I read about Stagedoor Manor in *The New York Times*," she told the British edition of *Esquire* in 2004. "It said it taught you how to become a 'theatre star.' I begged my parents to let me go." She was not the only one. Robert Downey, Jr., played Mr. Deusel in a 1976 Stagedoor production of *The Diary of Anne Frank*. Jennifer Jason

A young Natalie Portman starred as Sally Bowles in a 1995 Stagedoor Manor mounting of *Cabaret*. Years later, Oprah Winfrey played a clip from that production on her show.

Leigh starred as Amanda Wingfield in a 1977 production of *The Glass Menagerie*. Other Stagedoor alumni include Felicity Huffman (*Desperate Housewives*), *Two and a Half Men* co-star Jon Cryer (one of the highest-paid actors on television), Bryce Dallas Howard (*The Twilight Saga: Eclipse*), Mary Stuart Masterson, Josh Charles (*Sports Night*, CBS's *The Good Wife*), Shawn Levy (the director of the *Night at the Museum* films), and Amy Ryan (an Oscar nominee for *Gone Baby Gone*). In the 1990s, Ben Foster (*3:10 to Yuma*) and his kid brother Jon Foster (ABC's *Accidentally On Purpose*) attended together, at ages twelve and eight, respectively.

Lea Michele (a Golden Globe nominee for Fox's *Glee*) spent three summers at Stagedoor Manor. By the time she arrived at camp in 1998, she'd already been in *Les Misérables* on Broadway. Still, she says, "I never had a lead at Stagedoor. I was in a revue, *Side by Side by Sondheim*. I also sang the 'Pinball Wizard' solo in *Tommy*. My last summer, I was supposed to be one of the friends in *Sweet Charity*, but I left to do a workshop of *Spring Awakening* in New York." One couldn't exactly blame her. "It was a real job," she says. And? "I made money." *And?* "And I got to play the lead."

There are so many Stagedoor Manor alumni in Hollywood and on Broadway that the group has its own name: the Stagedoor Mafia. "I don't want to call it the Mafia," says the singer and actress Mandy Moore. "It's more like a secret society. It's this knowing look you get from people: Ah . . . Loch Sheldrake."

———

With so many success stories, the ground has shifted.* For those who aspire to a career in the performing arts, theater camp can increasingly be a stepping-stone. And the competition among the camps vying for these children's tuition money is more heated than ever. According to the American Camp Association, the number of accredited camps with an emphasis on arts education grew from 527 in December 2001 to 811 in June 2009, a jump of more than 40 percent. Peg Smith, the organization's chief executive, said the increase could be attributed in part to the elimination of school arts programs and the popularity of films like *High School Musical* and reality shows like *American Idol*. (Not to be left out, 19 Entertainment and Fremantle-Media, the companies behind *American Idol*, founded Idol Camp— where series castoffs like Bucky Covington instructed would-be teen sensations. However, in a testament to how difficult the camp business can be, despite the name recognition, Idol Camp folded after just a few summers.)

———

* This section (pp. 9–13) is adapted from *The New York Times*, July 27, 2008. Copyright © *The New York Times* All rights reserved. Used by permission and protected by the Copyright Laws of the United States. The printing, copying, redistribution, or retransmission of the Material without express written permission is prohibited.

Among the eight hundred camps, three are frequently cited as gold standards: Stagedoor Manor, French Woods, and Michigan's Interlochen Center for the Arts. Of that lot, Stagedoor Manor is the only one focused exclusively on theater. Stagedoor caps its enrollment at 290 children a session, and spots fill up nine months in advance; campers, from determined small-town tykes to Bruce Willis's daughter, are admitted first come first served (no audition required, with returning campers getting a first shot).

While the average overnight summer camp costs $400 to $700 a week, Stagedoor Manor charges closer to $5,000 for a three-week session. "Parents want to get quality for their money," says Jennifer Rudin, who spent several years as the director of casting and talent development for Disney Theatrical Productions and is a Stagedoor alumna herself.

To compete in this increasingly crowded marketplace, camps are expected to offer top-notch facilities and professional staff. Newer theater programs are courting high-profile teachers to compete with the better-established camps. The acting coach Howard Fine is one of the principal instructors at Deborah Gibson's Electric Youth, a new camp program based in Los Angeles. "We're living in the day and age of *American Idol,* where everything seems instant," says Gibson, the pop singer who made her Broadway debut in *Les Misérables* in 1992. "You can win your career on television. But you can't sustain it without the training." She added that she was able to recruit Fine by explaining to him that children are "just little adults."

Stagedoor Manor's reputation is global. In 2009, the camp attracted kids from forty-four states and from countries as far-flung as Thailand and France. Each summer, the camp's staff offers master classes in acting and voice. There are tutorials in makeup, lighting, and set design. And while it is tempting to think of a theater camp's artistic staff as some sad *Waiting for Guffman* sketch, the staff at Stagedoor is a mix of seasoned professionals and graduate students. In

2008, Jacob Brent directed *Rent* at Stagedoor; in the off-season, he helped cast the original Broadway company of *Billy Elliot*. Travis Greisler, another Stagedoor director, made his Broadway debut in *The Who's Tommy* at age nine and (more recently) assisted Tony nominee Michael Greif on a Manhattan workshop of a new musical, *Mrs. Sharp*, starring *30 Rock*'s Jane Krakowski. In 2009, Justin Mendoza—a Stagedoor Manor music director—had to leave camp early, because he was hired to do that same job for the national touring company of the Tony-winning musical *In the Heights*.

What distinguishes Stagedoor Manor isn't just the level of education, it's what they're teaching—and *how* they're teaching it. The Stagedoor Manor ethos: Learn by doing. Or more specifically, Learn by doing grown-up (and, some may say), age-inappropriate material. While a standard high school drama program might include chestnuts like *Fiddler on the Roof* and *Oklahoma!*, Stagedoor Manor pushes the envelope. The camp has showcased productions of Bertolt Brecht's *Caucasian Chalk Circle* and Federico García Lorca's "rural trilogy," which includes *The House of Bernarda Alba* and *Blood Wedding*. Not to mention a controversial Stagedoor presentation of *Carrie: The Musical*, a bloody cult piece that played a grand total of five performances on Broadway in 1988 before closing at a loss of $8 million.

"Stagedoor is a pretty special animal," says comedian and former camper Michael Ian Black (Comedy Central's *Michael and Michael Have Issues*). "It's a lavender animal. It's a lavender, sparkly, bedazzled animal. I played a smarmy child molester in *Runaways* at camp. There's a rape scene in that show. Theatrical kids are happy to enact rape scenes. They'll do whatever they're asked."

Besides top-notch training and envelope-pushing productions, there is now the chance to be *discovered*. These opportunities have increased exponentially in recent years, as visits to Stagedoor by casting agents and managers have become a more frequent fixture of the summer. In 2008, the composer Jason Robert Brown scouted children for his Broadway-bound musical *13* at Stagedoor Manor. Jennifer Rudin (formerly of Disney, now a talent manager) refers to Stagedoor as "one-stop shopping." Emily Gerson Saines, Cynthia Nixon's manager, signed the young actor Sebastian Stan after seeing him in a Stagedoor Manor class. (Having since made his Broadway debut opposite Liev Schreiber in 2007's *Talk Radio* and completed an arc on *Gossip Girl,* Sebastian Stan is now the rare young actor with both serious theatrical credibility and CW cachet.)

Many theater industry veterans say that precocious careerism has become more common among young performers. In 2006, the producer David Stone, an alumnus of French Woods (where he played Wilbur in *Charlotte's Web*), invited children from his former playground to see *The 25th Annual Putnam County Spelling Bee* on Broadway. Stone recalls a Q and A after the show: "These kids asked the most sophisticated questions. Like, 'How do you get an agent?' 'What's it like to do the show every day?' Questions about an actor's *process*."

The actress Bryce Dallas Howard isn't surprised at the precocious nature of this new generation—at French Woods or elsewhere. Bryce spent two summers at Stagedoor Manor in the 1990s. "Stagedoor is a camp of little grown-ups terrorizing each other," she recalls. "And it was fantastic."

The stakes, or the perceived ones at least, are rising exponentially for these campers. Larry Nye, Stagedoor Manor's director of dance and a professor at Southern Connecticut State University, shares a revealing anecdote: "At Stagedoor, we often have agents in to see workshops and performances. If someone strange walks in—and it could be the maintenance guy—and sits in the back of the theater, the kids will say, 'Who is *that*?'" Larry usually tells them it's an agent, even when it's not. "Anything to get a performance out of them!"

If there is any question that Stagedoor Manor has matured into a singular entity, this next anecdote should settle that. In 2006,

Courtney Love (reformed grunge queen, widow of Kurt Cobain) came to Loch Sheldrake to see her daughter, Frances Bean Cobain, in a production of the musical *Leader of the Pack*. "They gave my daughter a shit part," Courtney says. "She was in, like, some tertiary chorus line. It really pissed me off. The girls at camp called her horrible names. They were awful to her. I had to have Drew Barrymore—her godmother—call her at camp. I asked her to have them say over the PA system, 'Frances, you have a phone call from Drew Barrymore,' so the kids would stop making fun of her. But it was a character-building experience. Frances has been sheltered her whole life in Los Angeles. She had to stand up to these girls." Perhaps to inspire a little fear in the Stagedoor community, Courtney dressed up for the visit, so her presence would be known. "Honey, I was head to toe in red, you don't even want to know. I went as Joan Crawford." That wasn't the end of her theatrics. Not by a long shot. At lunchtime, Courtney got into a fight with a hot dog vendor who'd set up shop at camp for the weekend. Punk rock to the end, she tried to pay for her meal with a hundred-dollar bill. When the vendor refused to make change, Courtney Love threw up her hands in frustration and shouted: "Who do I gotta *fuck* around here to get a hot dog?"

Still, her daughter returned for a second summer. "She couldn't wait to go back," Courtney says. And the kid in Courtney Love understands why: "I wish I had a fucking Stagedoor when I was a child. I used to forge my parents' signatures so I could try to be the Rose Princess in Portland."

What really grabs you on a tour of Stagedoor Manor—what gets lodged in your throat—isn't the boldface names or quirky anecdotes. It's the graffiti. Backstage in the various theaters, campers armed with permanent markers have scrawled their names on the walls. In some cases, not just their names but wildly detailed résumés of their times at Stagedoor Manor. Skylar Lipstein: Judas in *Godspell* (2002). Jean Valjean in *Les Misérables* (2003). Guido in *Nine* (2004). Dana Steingold: Martha in *The Secret Garden* (1999). Sally in *Me & My Girl* (2000). Robin in *Smile* (2001). The Witch in *Into the Woods* (2002). These names are like comprehensive rosters from thirty years of campers—similarly disaffected theater geeks, pioneers, and talents who made a home in Loch Sheldrake.

As I walk backstage—at Stagedoor Manor's Elsie Theater, and then at the Jack Romano Playhouse—scanning the names of former campers, it occurs to me: while there are certainly plenty of recognizable names among them, many more are unknown. Stagedoor Manor is the proving ground, the place where talented kids from around the world come to test their skills and see how they measure up. Some will go on to long careers in the arts, others to fruitful work in vastly different fields. But while the camp's profile may have spiked in recent years, Stagedoor is not really the Mickey Mouse Club, churning out prefab stars. I think it serves a more important function, especially for those unknowns.

Summer camp is a crucible, a place where lasting personality traits are formed. Camp provides children with a place to experiment, a place to explore different aspects of their personalities in a safe environment. Such is the social import and merit of summer camp that social scientists have devoted lives to studying the effect of that two-month period—on self-esteem, on behavioral growth, on a host of variables.

But unlike other camps, at Stagedoor Manor teens and tweens are socialized to be *performers*—not jocks, or cool kids. The camp opens the door for them to a life onstage and makes real the possibilities that a high school star like me could only dream of. And in doing so, Stagedoor has changed the course of many lives, including Michael Ian Black's. The camp introduced him not just to a community of actors but also to his first manager. Black recalls signing with the manager

Shirley Grant after she spotted him in a Stagedoor Manor production. "She sat me down," he says. "I felt like a horse being inspected. She had me turn in profile. She was looking at my teeth. She was feeling my balls."

My visit to Stagedoor Manor as a journalist was an opportunity to observe a cross-section of aspiring performance talent, and to ask broad questions about what talent is—what defines it, who identifies it, how it is cultivated in this age of reality TV. In June 2009, I took three weeks off from my job as an editor at *GQ* magazine and moved into an outbuilding at Stagedoor Manor. During that time, I ate every meal in the camp's dining room. I sat in on rehearsals, tech meetings, late-night stitching sessions in the costume shop. I sat in the main office, the infirmary, the kitchen. I later interviewed nearly one hundred of the camp's alumni to trace the history of Stagedoor Manor, to piece together changing attitudes about the arts, about ambition, about sexuality.

I worried for some of these kids. I worried that the camp, simply by the nature of its success, set artificially high expectations: that if you worked hard, you could not only make a career of this, you could be a *star*. I wondered at the self-confidence (where does it come from?) these kids needed to carry on auditioning despite near-constant rejection. Because even successful actors, I found, still struggled with these concerns.

"When I was in my twenties, no one knew what to do with me," says Julia Murney, who attended Stagedoor in 1983 and 1984 and made her Broadway debut in 2005's short-lived musical *Lennon* before taking over the role of Elphaba in a celebrated turn in *Wicked*. "I wasn't an ingénue," Julia explains. "I wasn't a plucky young soprano at twenty-one. My tone, my bone structure, my visage—my everything was just more mature than my age. I got a lot of, 'Oh, you're neat. But we don't know what to do with you.' Once I got into my thirties, I could play those roles. And that was all great. And when things are starting to fly, you're surrounded by people who say, 'You're gonna do this and that! And fancy glittery unicorns are going to fly through the air!' It's thrilling. And you start to think, *You know what? Glittery unicorns might be really cool!*"

But as late as 2009, when she was appearing in a workshop of a Kander & Ebb revue with designs on Broadway, Julia was considering walking away from it all. "It's a weird life to subscribe to," she says. "It can beat the hell out of you. Right now, I'm in a spot where I'm thinking, *Do I want to keep doing this?* There's stuff I'd *like* to do in theater. But I've not necessarily felt like I'm gonna die if I don't get to."

To make matters worse for these aspiring thespians, all of the training in the world can still only get you so far. There is still that indefinable *thing* that, apparently, cannot be taught. "It is difficult to cast children," says Francesca Zambello, who directed Disney's *The Little Mermaid* on Broadway. "Theater camp can teach you craft, but you need that It factor." Or as Mama Rose says in *Gypsy*, "You either got it or you ain't."

Where did those unknown names from the backstage graffiti wind up? When the dream of a big Broadway opening turned into the (lesser) dream of regional theater, which gave way to the reality of bills and mortgage payments, did they look back at those head shots with regret? Or were those early head shots more like soccer trophies, which is to say souvenirs of a childhood time well spent?

I kept coming back to something Stagedoor's production director, Konnie Kittrell, told me. "Parents will call and say, 'Tell me the truth: Does my kid have any talent? Am I wasting my money? And I'll say, 'If your child finds something in this experience—finds an outlet they need, or finds self-confidence—how could you say it's wasted money?'"

And yet, there was hope—a spike in opportunities for child actors, and certainly more than enough to dangle a carrot. In 2008, a revival of *Gypsy* opened on Broadway with roles for seven children.

Billy Elliot, which opened in 2009 and may never close, employs seven boys plus a ballet class full of cutesy girls in pink tutus and tights. *Finian's Rainbow* opened in October 2009 with roles for three kids under the age of fifteen. And then there are the opportunities at Disney and Nickelodeon, networks whose original programming is now making household names out of America's camera-ready juniors in a way that was inconceivable even a decade ago.

Theater Geek is the story not just of a camp but of four decades of unique (and uniquely American) teenagers coming of age. For thirty-five years, Stagedoor Manor has asked for blood from its campers, and in return it has opened their eyes to a new worldview. When Stagedoor opened its doors in 1975, it was one of just a handful of summer camps devoted to the arts. Now, with hundreds of these camps out there, with Fox's *Glee* suddenly making it cool to perform in a troupe wearing matching vests, with gay high school kids (and even precocious middle school kids) coming out earlier—and without incident—what is the role of theater camp in this new era?

I spent the majority of my time at Stagedoor Manor with three campers—three exceptional teenagers in their final summer at camp before heading off to college. It was a unique snapshot, each of them caught between childhood and adulthood. I spent time with their casts, in rehearsals, and backstage before shows. I stayed so close because I was afraid I'd miss something important if I stepped away. But also because I fell in love with these kids, and was inspired by them—and their own acts of self-discovery—every day.

Amy B. Harris, a Stagedoor alumna and co-producer of HBO's *Sex and the City*, sums up the transformative power of a session at camp perhaps better than anyone else. "I was playing a homeless kid in *The Me Nobody Knows*," she says. "And I had a big monologue about being a druggie. I didn't shower for a week. I was trying to be Method about it. I'd have dirt under my fingernails and I'd think, *Good. That's what it'd feel like to be homeless!*" This was the early 1980s, and Amy's father was coming to visit for the performance, which was a minor coup: "I think my mom pushed him to let me come to camp. Before my dad saw me in *The Me Nobody Knows,* I think he thought of me as athletic and sporty. I remember thinking after the show, this was the first time he'd really *seen* me."

CHAPTER 1

It's Showtime

IN THE COZY LOBBY OF WHAT WAS ONCE A CATSKILLS HOTEL, nearly three hundred children sit, crammed in and anxious. It is day three at Stagedoor Manor, and in just a moment these campers will learn which roles they'll play in one of the thirteen shows to be produced in the next three weeks. And the wait—the interminable wait!—will be over.

The vibe in the wood-paneled room is tense, the subtext of every conversation: *God, I hope I get it.* Campers flit about. Some sing aloud to themselves as they walk. The kids refer to this unconscious vocal expression as "singing Tourette's," acknowledging that while the humming is certainly annoying, no one in this situation could reasonably be expected to control the sound any more than someone suffering from Tourette's syndrome could be expected to silence his outbursts. When theater geeks get anxious they also tap-dance. The actor Sebastian Stan (*Gossip Girl*) was a camper here not too long ago. He describes that moment when the cast lists go up. "It's nerve-racking," he says. "It's that same nervous adrenaline you find later in life after a professional audition, when you're waiting for that miracle phone call."

Stagedoor Manor campers have been known to cry on these mornings—both tears of joy and those born from seemingly life-ending disappointment. The musical's the thing. But not everyone can be cast in that session's hot show. "At Stagedoor, I was cast in *The Utter Glory of Morrissey Hall*," says Mandy Moore. "I think it was produced on Broadway once. It closed during intermission." (Actually, *The Utter Glory of Morrissey Hall*—a musical about a British headmistress, so popular at Stagedoor because it has an abundance of female roles—played seven previews and one performance on Broadway in 1979 before abruptly shuttering.)

The big show this session is still a secret. All thirteen titles are. And for three days these would-be thespians speculate, needle, debate. In an effort to rustle up some information on the still top-secret program, they badger the weaker staff members, pleading: "Just tell me what show *you're* directing." In fact, the anticipation was so terrible in 2009 that the night before the shows were revealed the entire camp was shipped off to the Middletown Mall to the movies. The off-grounds escape was meant to distract from the anxiety—*How many people does he need?*—not that it helped. "We talked about the shows the entire bus ride," says Rachael Singer, eighteen, who was beginning her final summer at Stagedoor. Over breakfast, on the morning the cast lists were to be posted, Rachael sat in the back of the cafeteria plainly nervous, mindlessly twisting a black hair tie in her hand and barely touching her food. If her friend Harry Katzman was similarly anxious, you wouldn't have known it by looking at his plate. It was licked clean.

———

Harry Katzman, eighteen, has dark curly hair, the ample physique of Zero Mostel, and the nearly translucent complexion of someone who spends an awful lot of time indoors. Two days earlier, walking into the lobby on the first day of camp, he was dressed in a striped T-shirt and pale blue jeans rolled up to the calf. He entered the space like Eva Perón in *Evita*, beckoning the peasants to him. Small girls approached Harry. Former co-stars and assorted hangers-on wrapped their arms around his body and hugged him tightly.

Harry is something of a celebrity at Stagedoor Manor—a teenager renowned for his rich voice, his good humor, and his always-reliable gossip. Justin Mendoza, one of the camp's music directors (he studied at the University of California–Irvine and spent three years as the associate music director at San Francisco's famous revue *Beach Blanket Babylon*), remembers meeting Harry in 2006. "Harry used to come up to me, grab my hand, and interlock our fingers," Justin says. "Then he'd want to *gossip*." Never shy, Harry fancied himself a musical theater expert—the cast albums on his iPod are sorted by West End versus Broadway company—and he thought nothing of handing out his unsolicited opinions to the camp's artistic staff. In 2006, Stagedoor's Raymond Zilberberg directed a production of *Company*, Stephen Sondheim's musical about open marriages and a lonely bachelor. As rehearsals began, Harry pulled the director aside and offered to lend him a DVD of the celebrated 1996 Donmar Warehouse production of *Company*, which Harry said had "some ideas I could borrow," Raymond recalls, shaking his head in loving disbelief.

Harry rarely keeps his thoughts to himself. On the first day of his first summer at Stagedoor Manor, Harry joined a conversation of returning campers who were busy discussing their audition songs. The boy to Harry's left said he was planning to sing "Dancing Through Life," from *Wicked*.

"I made a face," Harry admits. "I was such a jerk." For his part, Harry sang "Luck Be a Lady," from *Guys & Dolls*. Not exactly an inspired choice, he admits now. "But at least it was traditional!" If Harry came across, shall we say, *strong*, that summer, he had an excuse: "I was among my people for the first time."

Harry comes to Stagedoor from Columbia, South Carolina. And he is, in many ways, the archetypal Stagedoor theater geek—a small-town boy with an expressive personality who loves theater and finds a second home in Loch Sheldrake. Harry's mother, Debbie Katzman, does not mince words. "Stagedoor was Harry's savior," she says, preferring to leave it at that.

Harry wasn't always a star at camp. He'd turned in reputable performances before, notably as Thénardier in a 2006 production of *Les Misérables*. In a 2007 staging of *Grand Hotel*, Harry played Hermann Preysing, manager of a struggling textile mill who commits rape in act two. Harry's onstage verisimilitude was frightening. "He creeped us out!" says Konnie, the camp's production director and associate producer. Harry agrees with her assessment of his very fine work in *Grand Hotel*. After that show, he says, "people would legit not talk to me."

But nothing prepared the camp for Harry's turn as the Chairman in 2008's *The Mystery of Edwin Drood*. This lesser-known musical—not seen on Broadway since 1985—is a comedy of mistaken identities and murder, and the role of the Chairman is crucial to any production's success. First, it's the Chairman's responsibility to set the tone for the evening, encouraging the audience to be (as the script indicates) as "vulgar and uncivilized as legally possible." But the actor must also memorize reams of dialogue, not to mention craft an entirely separate role for the second act's play within a play. Yet, in a cast of Stagedoor Manor superstars, Harry put *Drood* in his back pocket and walked away with it. When he commanded, the audience laughed. Yet with a quick turn of his hand, he could inspire dead quiet. He pulled this performance off in three weeks—from a standing start? Dang, kid.

After *The Mystery of Edwin Drood*, Nancy Carson, a well-known New York talent agent who regularly scouts at Stagedoor, approached Harry. So did a rep from the talent agency Paradigm. "I got carded for the first time," Harry says. Business cards, he means. As in "Stay in

Harry Katzman played The Chairman in 2008's *The Mystery of Edwin Drood*. Harry spent a lot of time at the pool that session—not swimming, but rather studying his lines.

touch, kid. Let's work together." "It was flattering," Harry says, but also frustrating. "Nothing came of it. I live in South Carolina. I couldn't afford to fly to New York for auditions."

This display (otherwise thrilling) was another reminder of how geographically undesirable Harry was. There's not a lot going on for aspiring actors in Columbia, South Carolina, after all. During the winter months, Harry would sit up late at night—on e-mail, on iChat—living his life through a computer screen. He'd listen to stories from his Stagedoor friends, many of whom lived close to Manhattan, who were already auditioning for professional work. One of Harry's friends (spotted at Stagedoor by an agent) was up for the Meryl Streep film *It's Complicated* and then for the 2009 Broadway-bound revival of *Brighton Beach Memoirs*. Another Stagedoor contemporary, Aaron Albert (who'd understudied the lead in the musical *13* at the Mark Taper Forum in Los Angeles in 2007), auditioned for *Brighton Beach Memoirs* but didn't get the part, either. In the end, that role went to yet a *third* Stagedoor Manor camper, Noah Robbins, a phenom who's been dancing with Debbie Allen since he was six years old. Harry, at home in South Carolina, didn't begrudge his friends their success. But at times, listening to their industry talk left him frustrated and feeling further isolated.

There wasn't a soul in Columbia who didn't know Harry wanted to go to the University of Michigan. Harry had made that much perfectly clear. In recent years, under department chairman Brent Wagner, Michigan's musical theater program had become arguably the best in the country. Recent Michigan alums include Gavin Creel (a Tony nominee for the 2009 revival of *Hair*), Alexander Gemignani (Valjean in the recent Broadway revival of *Les Misérables*), and Celia Keenan-Bolger (*The 25th Annual Putnam County Spelling Bee*). Admission to Michigan's program is a near impossibility: six hundred students apply annually for twenty spots. Undeterred, in his senior year of high school Harry flew to Ann Arbor with his mom for the audition, which included two songs, a monologue, and a dance combination. "I don't dance," Harry admits. "I *fance*. I'm a *fancer*. I fake dance." Really? "I'm terrified of dancers," he says. "They can kick their face!" Still, Harry smiled through the choreographed portion of the morning, making his way across the stage, hoping some well-played jazz hands might distract the committee from his two left feet.

Eighty people auditioned for Michigan that day. Of those eighty, Harry Katzman was the only one accepted.

And yet.

Harry reflects on careerism and on a curious sentiment bubbling up among his peers—a generation reared on *Hannah Montana* and *American Idol*. "I feel like I may have missed out," Harry says. "These thoughts go through my head. *Why don't people know me yet? Why don't I have an agent?* Maybe I could have been on a Nickelodeon show. I've never had stage parents to make it happen. I'm doing this on my own."

Brian Muller, eighteen, is something of an anomaly at Stagedoor Manor. For one thing, his iPod is more Jay-Z than (Tony nominee) Jayne Houdyshell. Also, he's athletic.

Nearly six feet tall, with good hair and good teeth, Brian grew up on the Upper West Side, and he possesses that particular air of bravado that only comes from a childhood spent treating Manhattan as your own backyard. During his first summer at Stagedoor Manor, when Brian was eleven years old, he spotted a bunch of the older boys playing basketball on the camp's one-rim half-court. Brian ran at a clip to join them. But he was disappointed to find, upon closer inspection, that this was an *ironic* contest. "They were playing basketball," Brian says, "but as a joke. Like, Ha ha, Stagedoor kids playing sports." Brian grabbed the ball and shot a few from outside the key. He didn't make a single basket. "But at least I hit the rim," Brian says. "The other kids looked at me and were, like"—accusatorily—" 'Why are you *good* at basketball?' "

There's a famous scene in *A Chorus Line* where a young man steps forward to explain how he first started dancing. He says it began when he followed his sister to class one day. *"I'm watchin' Sis go pitterpat,"* he sings. *"Said, I can do that, I can do that."* That, in a lyric, is how Brian Muller wound up at Stagedoor Manor. Visiting his sister at camp years ago, he'd stumbled into the Stagedoor lobby, his eyes suddenly immense. He then spent the next ten months pleading with his parents to send him to theater camp. The Mullers were, to say the least, surprised by their son's sudden interest in the arts. At that young age the only thing Brian ever wanted to be was a professional golfer. Brian's father worked in the kitchen design business and certainly never expected this from his son. "My dad wasn't listening to Patti LuPone records at night," Brian says. Brian's childhood friends were, likewise, somewhat alarmed. "We all went to sports

Brian Muller stars in a 2004 production of *Oliver!*, playing the famously hungry orphan. Years later, Brian will reflect: "Why could I do a better cockney accent when I was eleven than I can now?"

camp," says his classmate Billy Greene. "We thought theater camp was weird."

Weird or not, the Mullers consented, enrolling their son for one three-week session in the summer of 2002. That was all it took. Brian fell in love with the place and, really, with the discipline of acting. And what started as a silly summertime adventure somehow snowballed into something more vocational. At twelve or thirteen, an agent picked Brian out of a Stagedoor rehearsal. She wanted to see him in New York when camp let out. But the Mullers hesitated. "What did we know about agents?" says Brian's mother, Nancy, now a communications officer at Bank of America. The Mullers waited to call longer than most parents of aspiring young actors would have. Finally they went to see this woman in her Manhattan office, where she asked Brian to sing a song and read a scene. "We can take this as slow as you want, or as quickly as you want," the agent told Brian's parents.

And so it began. Brian went on an audition for a Tostitos commercial, the one about kids at a slumber party. ("Shhh! Get the Tostitos," Brian had to say.) He went out for an independent film where he'd play identical twin brothers, one of whom gets killed in a fire. No luck there, though he did land a role in the workshop of a new musical, *Pages,* the story of a thirteen-year-old aspiring pornographer. What does Brian remember about that period in his life? The casting directors? The waiting rooms? The rejection? No. "When I smile," Brian says, "my left eye is smaller than my right. So in my first head shots, it looked like I had a lazy eye."

Brian returned to Stagedoor Manor every summer since that first and found his niche despite being something of a minority, both in athletic ability and attitude toward the dramatic. For example, in 2008, he starred in a Stagedoor Manor production of the southern drama *Dark of the Moon,* a sort of backwoods *Romeo and Juliet* about a girl in love with a witch-boy. In a beautifully affecting final scene, Brian cradled his co-star, Morgaine Gooding-Silverwood, in his arms as she lay dying. Unfortunately, when he laid her down, he placed her too close to the footlights, and her dress started to smoke. Midscene, the actress cracked one eye and whispered: "Am I on fire?"

"Yes," Brian replied stomping out the flames with his fist, before finishing the scene, to wild applause. Meanwhile, his co-star, a wonderfully talented actress, was inconsolable. "I was angry with myself for breaking character," she said.

"You were on fire!" Brian shouted in response.

Despite years of acting at home and at camp, when it came time to apply to college, Brian's mother Nancy was surprised her son homed in on Bachelor of Fine Arts programs. "As a kid, he'd leave an audition," she says, "and I'd ask him, 'How did it go?' He'd mumble, 'It was fine.' And that was it." Was it inertia carrying her even-tempered son through? "I mean, a BFA?" she asks. "What is *that*?" Brian's father convinced her that their son should at least apply to these programs. Though he probably wished his boy had chosen a more stable profession, "he's excited that I have a path," Brian says.

Brian's friends, that athletic bunch from Manhattan's Trevor Day School who'd initially deemed theater camp "weird," were likewise now on board. "I think Brian's agent used to work with Britney Spears," Billy says. "That's legit!" And they've come to embrace their friend's potential stardom. They even have a nickname for him: Vince. "Like on *Entourage*," Brian says, smirking. On that HBO series, Vince is the big Hollywood stud and a true ladykiller. It's not exactly a stretch. At Stagedoor in 2009, there was a teenage girl who admitted that the only reason she was there for session one was that Brian was coming for session one. The girl switched her own plans, she says, "for the chance to *kiss* Brian." (Except she didn't say "kiss.")

In the spring of his senior year, Brian was accepted into the prestigious acting program at Carnegie Mellon University. And he immediately took on the lax attitude of a high school senior with the next four years locked up. "I was going to Carnegie Mellon," Brian says. "I thought, *It's senior year and I can chill out. I'll go to college and it'll be awesome.*"

But in the same way that fate intervened when Brian, a ten-year-old aspiring golfer, stumbled into the Stagedoor lobby to visit his sister, once again some larger force would give Brian a nudge. It was around the time that his acceptance letter to Carnegie Mellon showed up that Brian auditioned for the national tour of *Little House on the Prairie*, a new musical starring Melissa Gilbert. A dance audition and a subsequent callback followed for Brian; and then a waiting game.

One spring night, he came home to find his parents and his sister seated at the kitchen table. Brian's father looked angry. "Did you leave my bedroom door open?" he asked. "Because the dog peed in my room—"

Brian: "I'm sorry, I thought it was closed."

Dad: "—and you got the job."

Elation. For the next hour, the family discussed logistics. The *Little House on the Prairie* company would start rehearsals in August 2009 before departing on a twenty-six-city national tour. Brian wondered if his parents would let him defer college. Was it even their decision to make? His dad, as rational as he'd always been, laid it out: "If this happened four years from now, after graduation, this would be the greatest thing, right? So why not do it?"

This was to be Brian's eighth (and last) summer at Stagedoor Manor. He is caught between two worlds, that push-and-pull between childhood and what comes next. It's all moving a bit quickly, isn't it? Graduation. A role in a national tour. He's heard about life on the road—and how lonely it can be. Too much free time. A different city every few weeks. In quiet moments, he worries: Would life ever be as good as this summer again? Surrounded by his best friends? Girls returning to camp simply for the *chance* of catching his attention? Couldn't he just hit pause and linger for a minute? Was he ready to be a working actor?

On day one at Stagedoor Manor 2009, the child in Brian wins out. Eighteen, handsome, with a helmet of brown hair, Brian stands at the lobby piano, leading a particularly spirited round of "Giants in the Sky," from the Sondheim musical *Into the Woods*. This particular song concerns Jack (of the beanstalk) and his adventures in the cloud kingdom where he meets a giant and his wife. In Brian's hands today—as befits his personality—the song takes on a slightly different meaning. When Brian sings the lyric, *"She gives you food and she gives you rest / She holds you close to her giant breast,"* he shouts "breast!" and seems very pleased with himself for being so clever.

What role would Brian play this session, his last at Stagedoor Manor? He had no clue. He wasn't even sure if he'd be in a musical or a drama. He circled "either" on his form, letting the camp decide, happy to put his faith in the system. Konnie—the head of the casting committee, a onetime actress and costume designer from the Smokey Mountains of Tennessee who has worked at Stagedoor for more than two decades—certainly knew him well enough to make that decision. She had something in mind for Brian. She had something in mind for everyone, as Rachael Singer would soon find out.

———

"The first two days at Stagedoor are the worst," Rachael Singer says.

Rachael, eighteen, is seated outside the camp's Playhouse Theater (once the hotel's disco) at 9 P.M. on day one, waiting to audition for the casting committee. It's an unseasonably chilly night, and she is wearing a black cotton dress, with a blue tie-dyed scarf wrapped around her neck. She shivers a bit, clutching a Styrofoam cup of tea. "Throat Coat!" she says, identifying her favorite brand of herbal elixir. "It's all we drink at Stagedoor."

Rachael, just five feet tall ("and a half!" she adds), with brown hair that falls an inch below her shoulders, is joined by the oldest girls at camp; each holds the sheet music for her audition, rustling the pages to relieve her nerves. As William Goldman writes in his landmark book *The Season*, "Auditions are degrading, humiliating, ineffective— and the best system yet invented for casting a play."

"I can't wait to get this over with," Rachael says.

Rachael might be short in stature, but her height is diametrically opposed to the size of her voice (the tremors she produces could raze buildings). Her father, a lawyer in Palm Beach Gardens, Florida, remembers the first time he heard his daughter sing. "When Rachael was eighteen months old," Mike Singer says, "we were in the car driving from Vermont to Montreal. The radio was on. Rachael's sitting in the back, singing along to 'Hey, Jude.' I couldn't believe it." And the girl never stopped. At age three she would dance around the house mimicking songs from *Fiddler on the Roof*. At five years old her dad looked into voice lessons. "It was tough to find a coach who would give voice lessons to a five-year-old," he says. Especially in South Florida. Meanwhile, Rachael's mother, Amy, is a speech pathologist, and she was concerned that intensive lessons at such a young age might damage her daughter's vocal cords. But after some due diligence, the classes were arranged. Parents often enroll their girls in ballet at the age of five, her father reasoned, so why not voice?

Growing up in the Sunshine State presents its own challenges for a would-be actress, but Rachael's parents did what they could. The girl performed with the Lakeworth Players, a community theater. If some nearby organization needed an adorable moppet to sing the National Anthem, Rachael was there. When her aunt died of complications related to diabetes, Rachael got involved with the Diabetes Research Foundation, singing at benefits whenever possible. In middle school, she opened for KC & the Sunshine Band. She sang for Donald Trump at The Mar-a-Lago Club in Palm Beach.

As a young teenager, she auditioned for the Dreyfoos School of the Arts, a magnet program forty-five minutes from home. Rachael's voice had developed a bluesy quality. And in the eighth grade, a teacher there pulled her aside to ask, "You do know you're not *black*, right?" Rachael loved the school, yet even in an intensive arts program, she never quite felt as if she could discuss her ambitions with her classmates. If she had an audition or an extracurricular performance, she sometimes told her friends that she had a family commitment that weekend, rather than go into detail and further separate herself from the pack. If Rachael had a complaint it was this: some of the students at Dreyfoos lacked a significant work ethic. No one at Stagedoor Manor questioned Rachael's work ethic.

For her first Stagedoor audition in 2006, Rachael sang "When You

Got it, Flaunt It," from *The Producers*. It's the song that introduces the Swedish secretary, Ulla Inga Hansen Benson Yansen Tallen Hallen Svaden Swanson; Uma Thurman played the part in the 2005 film. "The character is tall, blonde, Swedish, and beautiful," Rachael says. "Everything I'm not." (When Rachael utters this, over lunch before camp begins, her mother shakes her head, giving her daughter a troubled look, one that says *I've heard this before*, one that pleads, *Why can't you see what I see?*)

"I'm not legally a midget," Rachael adds. "At least there's that."

It is a hallmark of teenage years to feel betrayed by one's body. But this kind of insecurity is compounded for young actors, Rachael concluded. In the summer of 2008, the casting director for the Jason Robert Brown musical *13*, a then-Broadway-bound show about middle school brats in the Midwest, showed up at Stagedoor Manor to audition select campers. Rachael had three callbacks before she was cut. "Too old," the casting director wrote next to her name (on a piece of paper the girl was never meant to see). Too old? "Sweetie!" Konnie said, pointing to Rachael's chest. It wouldn't be the last time she heard that. When a scout for Broadway's *Spring Awakening* came to Stagedoor, Rachael auditioned but was labeled "too developed." Well, that was that. Over the winter, she worked hard to lose fifteen pounds, not an insignificant sum for a compact frame—much of it coming off the top.

If the professional opportunities weren't exactly panning out, they certainly kept coming. In 2008, Stagedoor Manor put up a production of Andrew Lippa's *The Wild Party*, a gem about two vaudeville performers on a cocaine-fueled bender in Manhattan. Lippa's musical (based on a Roaring Twenties poem by Joseph Moncure March) premiered off-Broadway in 2000, and while it has since been produced regionally and at colleges, Stagedoor's production would be the first licensed to teenagers. The composer himself doubted that such a risqué show as *The Wild Party* would be palatable for high school students, or really, the *parents* of high school students. But Konnie pursued the rights aggressively and, along with the camp's head of music, Jamie Mablin, worked closely with the composer himself and representatives from Music Theatre International to tailor the content.

In *The Wild Party*, Rachael was cast as Mae, the petite, bubbly bride of a dim-witted boxer played by a camper who was at least two heads taller than her, which was part of the joke. Dressed in a purple 1920s dress, her dark hair tucked under a platinum wig, Rachael was a revelation, cavorting around the stage with her man. "Show 'em your muscles!" Rachael shouted, in a high-pitched squeak. *"Show 'em your muscles!"*

Rachael Singer was cast as Mae, a petite spitfire in Andrew Lippa's musical *The Wild Party*. A scout from Disney Theatricals was in the audience for this 2008 Stagedoor production, and later invited Rachael to New York to audition for a new musical with designs on Broadway.

Lippa, whose next show, *The Addams Family*, was scheduled to open on Broadway in 2010, happened to be in the audience that afternoon. A lightbulb went off. He was working on a new musical, *Man in the Ceiling*, for Disney Theatricals and was in the midst of casting that show's workshop. Might this five-foot-nuttin' girl be right for the obnoxious older sister? And so, in the fall of 2008, Disney's Jennifer Rudin called Rachael and invited her to come to New York to audition for Lippa and Thomas Schumacher, the president of Disney Theatricals. There was a caveat, though. Before Disney went down this road, they'd need a commitment from Rachael's family. If the girl got the part, they'd agree to relocate to New York for the duration of the production, however long that might be. Rachael would have to leave high school (in her senior year, no less) and be tutored in Manhattan. Her parents discussed it. Dropping out of school? Uh, okay. Who would move with her? Could one of them even *afford* to quit their job? And what of Rachael's two younger siblings? Still, the opportunity was too good to pass up. Rachael and her father flew to New York in October 2008 to audition for *Man in the Ceiling.*

She didn't get the job.

Though just eighteen, Rachael is already brutally aware of how tough this business can be. She is young enough to have a favorite sweatshirt (a Day-Glo yellow item she's convinced is infused with magic restorative powers) yet mature enough to have someone with the keys to her career insinuate she's too busty. "I'm trying to figure out where I fit," Rachael says. "What my *type* is." At five feet tall, she reasons, she's not quite an ingénue, but more likely a character actress. In the fall of 2009, Rachael was scheduled to enroll at the esteemed Boston Conservatory to study musical theater. But the great character roles don't come around for an actress until her thirties—if then. Did she have the resolve to stick it out? To fight?

"I'm always doubting it," Rachael says. "I'm always terrified of the rejection. I don't know." Her father shares similar concerns. "I worry every day," he says. "Are we making the right decision?" Tuition and expenses for one year at The Boston Conservatory can run to $60,000. "The job prospects are not good," Mike Singer says. "The economics don't make sense. But I believe in her talent. And I want to give her that shot."

On that first night of camp, shortly before 11 P.M., Rachael steps out on the Playhouse stage to sing for Stagedoor's casting committee. It's dark in the 300-seat theater. Looking out into the audience, Rachael can see little more than shadows cast by the piano lamp. She chose sixteen bars of "With One Look," from Andrew Lloyd Webber's *Sunset Boulevard*. Tonight, it's not Rachael's best work. She flubs the lyrics, making something up on the fly. While her tone is clear, that's about all one can say of the audition. And Rachael, dazed and excused, takes the sheet music back from the piano player and shrugs, as if to say, "What was that?" before exiting stage right.

But the performance wasn't the problem. Konnie has known Rachael for close to five years, and is well aware of her talent. From Konnie's perspective, the problem is the *song* Rachael chose. Barbra Streisand often performs "With One Look" in concert, and this only confirmed Konnie's suspicions. "Rachael thinks she's Fanny Brice," Konnie says, referencing the awkward, offbeat heroine of *Funny Girl*. "Rachael is content to play short Jewish girls for the rest of her life."

And that won't do.

No, Konnie has her own plans for Rachael. Perched in front of the casting chart—an oversized piece of oak-tag listing every major role up for grabs that Stagedoor session—Konnie picks up her pencil and writes the number 150 in one of the small squares.

"Sometimes the numbers move," Konnie says. "But this one will stick."

CHAPTER 2

Beginners Showcase

ALMOST UPON ARRIVAL IN JUNE 2009, KONNIE KITTRELL dropped a bomb on these already wound-up campers. She had something unprecedented and ambitious planned for this session, she said: Stagedoor Manor would put up a Sondheim festival. "Six Sondheim shows!" she says. Upping the drama, publicity was expected, she said, with reporters making the trek to Loch Sheldrake from Manhattan. "Playbill.com will be coming," Konnie says.

The idea of a Sondheim festival for teenagers (*by* teenagers) is at once ludicrous and inspired. Stephen Sondheim is the most important composer-lyricist working in musical theater today, and his music is tricky business, all intricate, dissonant harmonies, many in minor keys, plus mouthfuls of complicated lyrics. This is the man who rhymed *liaisons* with *raisins* in *A Little Night Music*—and won a Tony for it. "I told Konnie she was crazy," Harry Katzman says with a laugh. "You may have enough talent to cast the leads, but you need to fill out the ensemble, too."

So, why Sondheim? For one, Konnie wanted to challenge these

kids—perhaps the most talented graduating class, collectively, the camp had seen in some time. But there was a secondary reason Sondheim might hold their attention. The rap on the composer is that his work is cold, arrogant even. But Sondheim is really a spiritual cousin to these theater geeks. His characters are desperate for emotional connections. "Being Alive" from *Company*, "Finishing the Hat" from *Sunday in the Park with George*—these are songs about unapologetic need. Bobby in *Company*, the bachelor who won't settle down, eventually begs, "*Somebody crowd me with love, somebody force me to care, somebody make me come through, I'll always be there, as frightened as you, to help us survive being alive.*" It's worth noting that Sondheim's first musical, *Saturday Night* (written at age twenty-three), was about a young man in Brooklyn aching to be touched. While Sondheim described himself as "the boy in the bubble" to his biographer, Meryle Secrest, like these kids, he wasn't a loner. As an undergrad at Williams College, he was so eager to fit in that he pledged a fraternity.

Konnie has given the graduating Stagedoor seniors—eighteen of 291, with Harry, Brian Muller, and Rachael Singer among them—each a chance to request a role in a specific Sondheim musical. In a sign of just how in-the-know these kids are when it comes to musical theater history, one smarty-pants camper cracks, "Can I be in *Road Show*?"—referencing a troubled Sondheim property that, after a decade in the woods, had a brief off-Broadway run in 2008. As if returning a well-played volley, another kid asks if he can do John Doyle's staging of *Sweeney Todd*; when Doyle directed that show in London and New York a few years back, he was applauded for bringing a new intimacy to the work by having the actors double as the orchestra, accompanying themselves onstage. "I should have brought my cello," someone jokes.

Still, Sondheim? On five stages? What sort of theater camp *is* this? To understand the ambitions of both Stagedoor Manor and its campers, to understand what need the camp fills in their lives, one must go back to the beginning—to the deranged, corrupt, unlikely, and heart-felt operation that first inspired Carl Samuelson to open Stagedoor Manor.

———

In the summer of 1971, a reporter from the *New York Times* traveled to a seemingly idyllic summer camp called Beginners Showcase, which was run out of an old homestead near Georges Mills, New Hampshire. The camp was in its fifth season and thriving. "With a brisk nod to the ancient Greeks," Howard Thompson wrote, "the youngsters were preparing a full-length outdoor *Medea*—flooded with strategic tree-lighting, on barbecue-pit rock slabs by a brook that trickles into Lake Sunapee." Thompson went on to describe the educational opportunities at Beginners Showcase, and the sheer determination he identified on the faces of these campers. "The big question at Beginners Showcase is simple and virtually unanimous: to act or not to act, professionally."

Dorothea P. Fitzmaurice, the executive director and co-founder of Beginners Showcase, explained the camp's mission to the *Times*: "What we offer is a thorough, accredited training setup where the kids can learn stagecraft, taste actual theater performing and then make up their own minds."

"With parental help," added Bob Brandon, the camp's president and director of admissions.

What the *New York Times* described was nothing short of a no-judgments summer stock for the next generation of talent waiting to (as people said then) tread the boards.

And from ten thousand feet, Beginners Showcase was utopia. Every few days, it seemed, a new show would premier at one of the camp's theaters. *Finian's Rainbow. Mame. The House of Bernarda Alba.* "I directed *A Funny Thing Happened on the Way to the Forum* in four days," says Peter Green, now a social worker in Rye, New York. "I don't know how it is possible, but I did it. We all did." At the time, the camp was unique in its ambitions. When Beginners Showcase Theatre and Music School/Camp, Inc. first opened its doors in 1967, it was one of just ten U.S. summer camps devoted to the dramatic arts. (By 2009, there would be more than eight hundred offering such programs.) And there was much to be admired about the place. The choreographer, Thommie Walsh, who later appeared in the original company of *A Chorus Line* on Broadway, taught dance at Beginners Showcase. Sally Lee, who'd danced in the film version of *The Music Man*, was imported from New York to choreograph a production of *Cabaret*. Despite the talented staff Beginners Showcase attracted, theater camp wasn't yet a finishing school for Broadway or Tinseltown. The campers didn't expect to be seen by the right people. That wasn't in their vocabulary, because there was no precedent. "There was no sense that you might be *discovered* at Showcase," says the playwright Nicky Silver, a Showcase camper in the 1970s who later contributed a new book to the 2002 Broadway revival of *The Boys from Syracuse*. "There were no agents or casting directors passing through." With that, he pauses, apparently to muster the dirtiest analogy possible with which to characterize that era at Beginners Showcase. "If you were talented," he says, "you might get a blow job behind the theater; if you weren't talented, a hand job."

It wasn't just Beginners Showcase's bona fides that attracted these campers, or the glossy brochure promising "a summer guidance training program . . . at an altitude of 1,200 feet." To be blunt: these kids often enrolled because no one else would have them. "At Showcase, you weren't going to be ridiculed because you liked to sing in public, or you were moody, or you threw tantrums," says David Edelstein, now the film critic for *New York* magazine, then Fagin in a Showcase production of *Oliver!* "You might not be especially charismatic or well liked or talented. But you were now a part of that great theatrical community." What these kids were searching for, desperately, was some confirmation that they weren't alone. "In high school," Edelstein says, "you'd walk into a rehearsal room and all of your defenses would fall away. At Showcase, it was like that for a full eight weeks."

Ronald W. Weich, whom President Obama appointed assistant attorney general for the Office of Legislative Affairs at the Department of Justice, was a Showcase camper, perhaps despite his father's wishes. "My father was never quite comfortable with us going to theater camp," Weich says. "He'd say, 'My friends go visit their children at camp, and their kids run to greet them in the parking lot carrying footballs and baseball bats. But you and your brother run to meet me in leotards and tights, coming from your dance class.'"

Still, these exasperated parents, it seems, were so relieved to find a place where their children belonged that they happily paid a then-wild sum of $1,150 in tuition for the eight-week program. "There was this network of parents," explains Charles Busch, a former camper and Pulitzer Prize–winning playwright of *The Tale of the Allergist's Wife*, "who didn't know what to do with their *sensitive children*. But they heard through the grapevine that there was this wonderful place where your *creative young boy* will feel at home. And they didn't do much investigation. They just sent him there."

"There was no swimming," Busch adds, as if further explanation were needed to separate Beginners Showcase from traditional summer camps in the area. "You were rehearsing all the time. The camp was this microcosm of showbiz—with stars, and hangers on, and wannabes, and power brokers." Without missing a beat, Busch, who has made a career of performing in drag, adds this assessment of his own status at Showcase: "I was a B-movie actress. I could never quite get into the prestige picture."

———

But all was not well in Glocca Morra.

Presiding over this supposedly idyllic scene was one Bob

Brandon—full name Robert Brandon Fuller—a man who should not have been entrusted with the welfare of children. And yet there he was making recruiting trips on behalf of the camp, dropping in on prospective Showcase families in the tri-state area. Among the many suspect claims Bob made was that he'd been the original Ronald McDonald clown. "He showed up at my house with photographs of himself dressed as Ronald McDonald," Edelstein says.

"That was the claim that made the camp legitimate," adds Richard J. Allen, now the head of the film, television, and digital media department at Texas Christian University. "That Bob Brandon had been Ronald McDonald."

In that 1971 *New York Times* article about Beginners Showcase, Bob Brandon talked a mouthful about the importance of "parental help." But help or supervision wasn't exactly his forte. Bob was quick with a balloon animal, and made frequent appearances at area birthday parties performing under his clown name, Tickles. The problem came when Tickles would return to Showcase drunk, still in full clown makeup. A former camper recalls Bob Brandon—overweight, gay, with a nasal falsetto voice approaching Truman Capote's—walking into a dorm room for young girls and making this lewd comment: "Flip 'em over and they all look the same."

If nothing else, Bob, who claimed to have written a book called *Sawdust and Lace: The Confessions of a Gay TV Clown*, was of a piece with the era at camp. "Beginners Showcase was a hotbed of sex and drugs," says Nicky Silver. "There was a group of people—ages twelve or thirteen—who thought they were *decadent*. As far as I can tell, everyone was stoned and having sex."

It's worth pausing to take the temperature of that time outside the camp's walls. The Vietnam War raged on. The musical *1776* was a hot ticket on Broadway. But when the cast of that show was invited to the White House to perform for Richard Nixon, the president's staff insisted the producers agree to drop an antiwar number first. (The producers balked; only when Nixon subsequently caved—he must have really wanted to see *1776*—did the cast travel to D.C.) Meanwhile, *Hair* transferred to Broadway's Biltmore Theatre where Leonard Bernstein walked out of an early performance. Richard Rodgers publicly trashed that show, too. But they were out of step with the public and *Hair* ran for more than four years. (True to that show's trippy roots, the creative team made no secret of hiring an astrologer to assist in casting.)

This was the era in which Beginners Showcase thrived. Andy Halliday, now a New York City performer and director, was a camper in the early 70s. He recalls a female counselor blissed out on LSD coming home late one night dressed in a devil's costume, presumably borrowed from the camp's costume shop. Standing atop a stairwell, this she-devil cackled, hurling a five-foot plastic pitchfork at a young girl's head. There were other staffing issues. The camp's owner hired a veteran performer (once a chorus boy in the Broadway production of *Blossom Time* in 1919) to teach exercise classes on the lawn. This man, well into his seventies, lived in his own house on a hill overlooking the camp, where he'd often invite young boys up to take baths.

It was chaos. The appeal of any training program is that it's a safe environment to make mistakes. But not so at Beginners Showcase, where tickets were regularly sold to the public and the camp's productions were reviewed by the local newspaper. And reviewed harshly! In 1970, Pulitzer Prize winner Charles Busch's best friend was cast as Og in *Finian's Rainbow*. "He was the most neurotic, vulnerable kid," Busch says. "He had asthma. He was adopted. And this asshole from the Lake Sunapee *Bugle*—or whatever the paper was called—referred to him as *too effeminate to play a leprechaun*. A gay slur in the newspaper. At fourteen!"

Oddly, these newspaper clippings were read like tea leaves by the camp's staff. In that same 1970 review of *Finian's Rainbow*, the writer for the *Daily Eagle* singled out the performance of a chorus girl, Roberta Dent, who was apparently burning with talent: "It was not long into the first act when the audience started to notice a young girl in the chorus with large black eyes . . . who had a large voice for such a little girl. She had no lines to read in the first act but her singing and her enthusiasm came through. By the time she appeared in the second act and had some lines to read and solo singing, the audience could not get enough of her. This girl, Roberta Dent, will bear watching." Two weeks after that review appeared in the newspaper, Roberta Dent was asked to star as Sally Bowles in a Beginners Showcase production of *Cabaret*.

"She was plucked out of the chorus line," Busch says. "A star is born!"

But the troubles at Showcase were not limited to newspaper reviews (or gay slurs, or the sexual exploits of the staff, or LSD for that matter). In 1974, two or three days into the summer—the same summer Nixon resigned—Bob Brandon disappeared from camp. No explanation was given. Months later he surfaced, armed with a new plan: he was moving Beginners Showcase from New Hampshire to Great Barrington, Massachusetts, where the camp would operate under a new name (never a good sign for a business), *Berkshire* Showcase. Beautiful new buildings were under construction! he raved. Not surprisingly, two weeks before the campers were due to arrive, in June 1975, that plan was abruptly scrapped. "Something about permits," says Peter Green, who worked at Showcase at the time. Bob Brandon scrambled to find a new location, ultimately renting out a property in Windham, New York—a full three hours from Great Barrington. Which, by the way, is how a camp called Berkshire Showcase opened in the *Catskills*.

Todd Graff (who later made a cult film called *Camp* based on his summer theater experiences) was a camper that first summer in Windham, where he was joined by future notables including Jeff Blumenkrantz (the original Broadway company of *Into the Woods*) and the culture critic Douglas Rushkoff. Todd describes the facilities in Windham, mockingly, as "this clapboard old Pepperidge Farm kind of structure."

"There was a scabies epidemic that first summer," Todd says. Worse, the water smelled terribly of sulfur—so much so that the children often opted to bathe in a nearby creek rather than hold their nose in the shower. (You'd see them walking down the road with bottles of shampoo in hand.) There were other concerns. The boy's dorm was not equipped with fire escapes, and after a routine inspection, the fire department shut the building down. "Rather than bringing the dorm up to code," Todd says, "Bob Brandon had the scenery shop build *wooden* fire escapes and attach them to the building."

Which begs the question: Where were the parents? Well, Todd Graff recently found a photo of himself in a production of *Cabaret* from the 1970s. He was fourteen years old. The show was directed by "a lesbian studies major," Todd says, and she created a role specifically for him: "I was the emcee's boy, and I was dressed in women's clothing and a dog collar. The emcee would walk me around the stage, and I'd sit there at his feet, gently stroking his thigh. That was my part." What disturbs Todd most about this photograph is that his *mother* took it. Shouldn't she have been concerned? "Oh, she was like, 'He's having a good time! So what if he's dressed in drag and a collar and leash and he's stroking another boy's thigh,'" Todd says. "It was such a different era."

Berkshire Showcase may have had a new name, and a new home, but it was operating under the same old troubled leadership, and its days were numbered. Bob Brandon would sit in the camp office dodging phone calls from creditors. "Fuck 'em!" he'd shout, in that nasal voice of his, in clear earshot of the campers. Actress Casey Williams appeared in a 1975 Showcase production of *Stop the World—I Want to Get Off*. The props had been rented. During rehearsal one day, she recalls strangers showing up to pry them out of the children's hands. "Things were being repossessed all around us," Casey says. The counselors had rental cars. "They weren't being paid for, either. There was a truck that disappeared."

Panic set in among the staff. "You needed the inside scoop to know to ask for your paycheck early," says Carin Zakes, who was a director that summer of 1975. "There wasn't enough money to go around." One afternoon, a woman nicknamed Mama Sally, sensing the growing unease among campers, threw on a feather boa, pulled the kids together in one of the theaters, and led them in a sing-along of "Everything's Coming Up Roses," from *Gypsy*. ("And *that* is how you make a kid gay," says Nicky Silver with a laugh.)

Keith Levenson, later the music supervisor for the 1997 Broadway revival of *Annie*, was a piano player at Berkshire Showcase. He was just fifteen or sixteen years old then, but he manages to look back on this time as an invaluable lesson. "In show business," he says, "you'd always be working for some producer whose check you'd be afraid would bounce."

Jeffrey Zeiner, an acting coach in Manhattan, knew Bob Brandon well, and after all these years he finally explains the fuzzy math that led to the demise of Berkshire Showcase—which didn't suffer for customers. "Bob Brandon took this glorious Upper East Side apartment," Zeiner recalls. "He took all the down payments from the campers and put it into this pretentious apartment. He bought thousands of dollars of furnishings. And then he ran out of money." (Bob Brandon passed away in 2005, nearly three decades after leaving Showcase. Over the years, he'd have several run-ins with the law—minor incidents such as passing a bad check for a couple hundred dollars—but in April 1985, he did manage to make national news as the subject of a tabloid-friendly case, in which a disgruntled mother allegedly hired him to dress up as Tickles the Clown and plant a cream pie in the face of a

Fairfield, Connecticut, school dean. The *Associated Press* headline: COUPLE ACCUSED OF SENDING IN THE CLOWN, BRIBING HIM.)

Showcase would not survive the summer of 1975. But there were so few arts camps in the country at the time, and most of those were dedicated to music. What would happen to these kids? Where would they go if Showcase closed?

––––––––––

Jackie Ferber was the camp director at Berkshire Showcase during the summer of 1975, and she knew just how dire the situation was even before the props were repossessed. That summer, Jackie—famous for her pink lipstick and deep tan—invited her good friends Carl and Elsie Samuelson up to visit. The invitation may have started as a social call, but it turned into a lifeline. The kids have to be fed, the counselors have to be fed, and there's no money, she told Carl and Elsie.

Carl was a jack-of-all-trades, a graduate of New York's DeWitt Clinton High School and then City College, who'd wanted to fight in World War II but was stationed in Virginia. In 1960, he and his wife, Elsie—hardworking folk of Bronx stock, who'd met on a blind date—moved to New Rochelle with their two daughters, ages seven and eight, in tow. "My mother didn't even drive at the time," says their daughter, Cindy Samuelson. When Jackie called, Carl was working in construction, overseeing projects in New Jersey.

Touring Berkshire Showcase, though, this builder from the Bronx had a shocking epiphany: he wanted to take over the theater camp. "I can't let this place go out of business," Carl told his family. And what started as a casual conversation over dinner soon grew heated. "My mother and I looked at him and said, 'You've gotta be kidding,'" recalls Debra Samuelson, the elder of Carl and Elsie's two daughters, who had just graduated from college at the time. It wasn't just that Carl, an entrepreneur at heart, lacked camp experience (though he had worked at a day camp once). He'd never worked in *theater* before.

He was a fan, and certainly appreciated the arts. He and his wife took their daughters to see Zoe Caldwell in *The Prime of Miss Jean Brodie* on Broadway, and to see other serious dramas over the years. "But we didn't have much money," Debra says. "If I saw one show a year over Christmas, that was it."

Cindy, herself an artist, had just graduated from the University of Wisconsin–Madison with a BFA. She knew the types of people her father regularly dealt with in the construction business, and she had an appreciation for the very different folk he would soon encounter. She turned to her father: "Do you really want to get involved with *theater people?*"

CHAPTER 3

Week One

IN A HEARTBEAT, RACHAEL SINGER WILL STAND BEFORE THE just-unveiled cast lists, so in shock that her command of nouns and verbs will break down completely. She will stare dumbfounded at the names up on the wall, making sure she's read the type correctly. She will once again trace her finger across the page, from left to right, from her name to that character's name. Rachael's face is blank, gone white suddenly, and she takes a step back, covering her mouth with her hand.

"I'm not," she says, trembling. "I'm not!"

———

Of the nearly three hundred campers here this morning—this third day of camp, the day the cast lists will be posted—some ninety-three have never attended Stagedoor Manor before. These are the faces to watch. One wishes to stand beside these newbies just to bask in the reflected glow of their unabashed, unironic joy.

The shows will be announced today, in an elaborate pantomime known as the Reveal. And the entire camp crowds into the lobby. White, stackable plastic chairs cover every inch of carpet, and as Konnie Kittrell appears onstage, the tension—thick as the humid summer air—mounts considerably. The anticipation is suffocating. Mercifully, she and the camp owner begin on schedule, shouting, "What time is it?" To which the kids reply, "It's showtime!"

One by one the directors emerge. Jeff Murphy, an educator and Liza Minnelli impersonator in the off-season, is joined onstage by his music director, who is busy theatrically eating a piece of pie. A ripple of recognition passes through the campers (who know a Sondheim reference when they see one). "In the Elsie Theater," Konnie shouts, "Jeff Murphy will be directing *Sweeney Todd!*"

And it's deathly quiet again. Chris Armbrister, the camp's program director, who has an MFA from the University of Alabama and dresses exclusively in Hawaiian shirts, appears from stage right, walking on tiptoe, leading a pack of staff members around the lobby. "Shhhh," he says, pointing off stage left, beckoning his band of merry men to follow him . . . *"Into the woods!"* Each of the thirteen directors will have a chance to introduce his or her show, performing a short skit, a juggling act, whatever they'd like, really. The Reveal is meant to be entertaining, but it serves a secondary purpose: it gives the individual staffers a chance to demonstrate their personalities. So if a camper winds up cast in something as obscure as *The Utter Glory of Morrissey Hall*, when they desperately wanted to be in *Les Misérables*, their excitement for that show's director—and his juggling act— might just cushion the blow.

Rachael Singer, Harry Katzman, Brian Muller—they've milked their sources dry and already guessed half the shows. Just one thing catches them truly by surprise this morning: for the first time in Stagedoor Manor history, this session the camp will produce fourteen shows, instead of the now-customary thirteen. "There were so many kids interested in dramas, we had to add a show," Konnie announces. She wasn't feeding them a line. At that very moment, a director was on a plane from the West Coast to Loch Sheldrake to direct the World War II drama *Cry 'Havoc'*, a last-minute addition to the program.

Finally, it's official: Stagedoor's first Sondheim festival will include *Into the Woods, Sweeney Todd, West Side Story, A Funny Thing Happened on the Way to the Forum, A Little Night Music,* and a revue, *Side by Side by Sondheim.* Rounding out the rest of this session's program is *Children of Eden, The Who's Tommy, The Drowsy Chaperone, The Children's Hour, Grease, The Young and Fair, A Midsummer Night's Dream,* and *Cry 'Havoc'.*

And then it happens. The smallest kids are dismissed first, taking off in a sprint. Rachael is pushed aside by a pack of rugrats. Kids are screaming around her. "I'm in *Tommy*!" "I'm in *Drowsy*!"

Rachael, dressed in a black cotton dress, finally makes her way up to the glass. She nervously twists a hair tie in her hand as she stands in shock before the lists. She expected to be cast as the Baker's Wife in *Into the Woods*, a role comfortably in her range, both vocally and stylistically. But she wasn't cast as the Baker's Wife. Nor was she cast as the ingénue, Janet van de Graaf, in *The Drowsy Chaperone.* Physically, Rachael didn't fit the part, she acknowledged that. But Janet is a tap-dancing role, and Rachael has excelled in those before at Stagedoor.

Instead, she stares at the list, confused, desperate to block out the commotion around her as she scans the names one last time. Gasping for air, she finds the words, whispering almost under her breath: "I'm Mrs. Lovett?"

———

If the prospect of an eighteen-year-old Mrs. Lovett doesn't at least put a smile on your face, pull up a chair. Because Lovett may be the most demanding role in the Sondheim canon, distaff or otherwise.

Sweeney Todd is the story of a British barber banished to an Australian prison for a crime he didn't commit. Fifteen years on he escapes, returning to London in a frantic search for his wife and daughter. Early in the show, he stumbles into Mrs. Lovett's pie shop, where a decrepit woman bakes the "worst pies in London."

This Mrs. Lovett, she's obsessed with Sweeney Todd (real name Benjamin Barker). Always has been, always will be. So much so that when Barker was deported—for what was meant to be a life sentence—she kept his razors tucked away in a closet. You know, on the off chance he might escape. Lovett is so drunk on this man that when he returns to London, starts calling himself by the name Sweeney Todd, and quits cutting hair—choosing to slit throats instead—she doesn't just stand by her man, she concocts an ingenious plan to dispose of his victims: She'll bake the cadavers into pies. Angela Lansbury originated this role on Broadway in 1979, and murder she *wrote*. With her soft-boiled eyes peeking out from beneath a wig of orange yarn, it was like watching a real-life crazy person on stage, armed with a rolling pin and bleached flour.

That Lovett is really an acting piece makes Rachael Singer an unorthodox choice. At Stagedoor, she'd excelled in shows like *Me and My Girl* and *42nd Street*—both tap dancing roles. Yes, she diversified in 2008, playing the title role in *Aida*. But that part calls for all the nuance of Steve Urkel. No one expects depth and character from Aida. They just want that Nubian freedom fighter to belt the crap out of Elton John's schlocky score and get off the stage.

In the fall, Rachael would begin her schooling at Boston Conservatory, trading four years (and nearly $240,000) for a possible lifetime of rejection. But first Konnie wants to test her, to see how she might do serving up, as Sondheim wrote, *"shepherd's pie peppered with actual shepherd on top."* "It's Rachael's last summer," Konnie says. "And I want to challenge her."

Ten minutes after the cast lists went up, Rachael was seated in the

Rachael Singer in the title role of Elton John's *Aida*, clutching the captain of the Egyptian Army, Radames (Daniel Fuentes).

camp's Elsie Theater (a 300-seat proscenium and perhaps the most prestigious space on grounds) clutching the *Sweeney Todd* script in her hands. She's turning the pages, but doesn't seem to be reading the words. It's the fear settling in.

And it must be said: Rachael Singer struggles from minute one.

The daily schedule at Stagedoor Manor is as follows: Breakfast at 8:30. Rehearsals start promptly at 9 A.M. Lunch is followed by two classes (maybe master acting, stage combat, ballet), then an afternoon recreation period and yet a third class. After dinner, each cast convenes for an additional two-hour rehearsal ending at 8:45 P.M. A nighttime activity—a movie, a dance—is on offer before campers are due back in their rooms for a 10 P.M. curfew. And then it begins again the next morning.

In a private lesson with *Sweeney Todd*'s music director, Justin Mendoza, Rachael wraps her five-foot-tall frame tightly in her sweatshirt, as if the atomic neon fabric might protect her from the challenge ahead. They are working on Mrs. Lovett's entrance, a song called "The Worst Pies in London." The song does not sit naturally in the sweet spot of Rachael's voice. And she stumbles through it, switching from chest voice to head voice indiscriminately. When she sounds too pretty, Justin cuts her off.

"I want it to sound *ugly*," he says, seated at the piano.

"Why?" Rachael asks.

Mrs. Lovett is preparing pie crust in a flea-ridden bakery in the wrong part of London Town. That's why. Justin strains to come up with a vocal direction that will help Rachael understand what he's hinting at.

"You know how Kristin Chenoweth sings?" Justin asks. "You know how she talks? Like a bratty school girl, *Nah nah nah nah nah nah.*" Rachael imitates him, imitating Chenoweth. "Use *that* voice," Justin says. He sings Mrs. Lovett's lyric pinched through his nose: *"These are probably the worst pies in London."*

It's not just the specific tone quality that's a challenge for Rachael. "The Worst Pies in London" is set in Lovett's bakery and Sondheim has written specific beats into the song where this woman is supposed to slap down some dough, pound the table with her rolling pin, or shoo away an errant cockroach. For example, Lovett notices Sweeney Todd entering her shop, and, holding her knife in the air, she screeches: "A customer! *Wait! What's yer rush? What's yer hurry?* (She sticks the knife into the counter) *You gave me such a—* (She wipes her hands on her apron) *fright. I thought you was a ghost. Have a minute can'tcher? Sit!"* And so on.

Rachael doesn't have props at this rehearsal, so the music director asks her to shout "Uh!" on the action beats.

"Wait! What's yer rush? What's yer hurry? Uh! You gave me such a —Uh! fright. I thought you was a ghost. Half a minute, can'tcher? Sit! [bang the rolling pin] *Sit ye down! Uh! Sit!"*

When Rachael makes a mistake, which she does often today,

she lets out an awkward giggle. Or throws her hands up in the air, comically shaking her fists at the sky. If she strains to get the words out, she should take comfort in the fact that Patti LuPone, famous for blurry diction, worked through similar troubles when she played the role on Broadway for John Doyle. (At least Rachael didn't have to accompany herself on the tuba.)

Still, she was making progress. In front of the piano, anyway, with no one watching. But at rehearsal, later that first week, standing in front of the twenty-three-member cast in Studio D—a mirrored room with fluorescent lighting—it's as if that afternoon session never happened. Rachael runs "Worst Pies," holding her script in her hand, yet she appears hopelessly adrift. The director, Jeff Murphy—a Stagedoor veteran some kids call Jeffles—asks to move on to her next song, "Poor Thing." At this point in act one, Sweeney Todd has returned from Australia, and he wants to know why the barbershop above Lovett's bakery has remained dark all these years. Mrs. Lovett, not yet recognizing Sweeney (much changed after fifteen years in prison), explains that the townspeople believe the place is haunted. *"There was a barber and his wife,"* she sings, *"and he was beautiful. A proper artist with a knife, but they transported him for life."* She then delves into the story of how an allegedly respectable Judge and his cohort took advantage of Sweeney Todd's young wife many years ago. The song is told in flashback, and Mrs. Lovett narrates while the ensemble reenacts the horrors perpetrated against Sweeney's bride.

Here, the director instructs the seventy-five-pound girl playing Sweeney's wife to lie down on the floor of the studio. He's moving through the scene at a brisk pace. Until, that is, a young cast member interrupts the proceedings with a question about Jeff's blocking. He wants to know why the character of Judge Turpin is suddenly lying on top of this innocent girl.

Jeff Murphy: "Get on top of her. But don't put any pressure."

Boy: [innocently] "Why is he getting on top of her?"

Jeff: "He's just getting on top of her."

Boy: "But why?"

Jeff: "He just is."

Boy: "But . . ."

Jeff: "He's raping her, Okay?"

Boy: [silence]

Rachael lets out a laugh. It's a rare moment of levity for the girl who was suddenly saddled with the near-impossible task of creating the role of Mrs. Lovett from scratch in two and a half weeks. Had she even *seen* the show before? Rachael shrugs. "I saw the movie with Johnny Depp."

Further complicating matters for Rachael, the camper playing Johanna, Sweeney's daughter, inhabits her character from the get-go. Johanna has been locked away by Judge Turpin. And the young actress playing the role, a girl named Dani Apple, was perfectly cast. Like Johanna, Dani has an ethereal look to her eyes that lends itself perfectly to the task. The campers take notice of her talent immediately. "She's a star," says Jordan Firstman (Sweeney Todd). And when Dani sings through "Green Finch and Linnet Bird," Jordan insists that the entire room quiet down, shouting: "Everyone listen! Dani Apple is singing!"

Rachael, looking on, is awed by the angelic sound of this girl's voice but forgets for a second that Johanna is supposed to sound gorgeous. Or that no one ever leaves a good production of *Sweeney Todd* talking about Johanna. Mrs. Lovett is *the* role. Still, exiting the rehearsal, Rachael grabs on to the music director's arm for support, pleading: "Will you work with me every day?"

Like any exclusive establishment, Stagedoor Manor has a clearly defined social hierarchy. Nowhere is this more evident than in the dining room. (Sebastian Stan, a Stagedoor alumnus who made his

Broadway debut in a 2007 production of *Talk Radio,* likens the cafeteria here to a minefield, referring to the ever-changing seating chart as "high-powered drama.") The cool place to sit this session is the Garden Room—a small, private dining space off the main cafeteria, hidden from the watchful eye of the camp administration. And the room is cozy, with barely enough floor space to accommodate two long tables and an upright piano. Naturally, this is where Rachael Singer, Brian Muller, Harry Katzman, and much of the talented, older campers eat lunch.

It is a raucous place. And though Rachael is largely silent today—preferring to wallow in her grilled cheese—the conversation otherwise ricochets back and forth. Topic one: Aaron Albert, a seventeen-year-old camper, who will be leaving Stagedoor in two weeks to film a new Disney XD series about a once-famous '80s rock band reinventing itself with a high-school-age lead guitarist. Aaron, who is working steadily, recently did a guest spot on Nickelodeon's wildly popular series *iCarly,* and there's now a rumor going around camp that he hooked up with that show's star, Miranda Cosgrove. Aaron, here eating a sandwich, sharply denies this suggestion, shouting: "She came over my house for a party. But that's it!" Other lunchtime topics include: the surprising popularity of jean shorts for men ("jorts"), the lack of attractive male campers this summer, and the women of Bravo's *Real Housewives of New Jersey.* After a while, one might think the only thing these kids talk about is *The Real Housewives of New Jersey,* but one would be mistaken. They also talk about *The Real Housewives of Atlanta.*

But the conversation, as always, returns to the shows and the progress of rehearsals. Someone asks Rachael about *Sweeney Todd,* about the Cockney accent she'll need to play Mrs. Lovett. Rachael brushes the question aside. She'd done a Cockney accent three years ago in a Stagedoor production of *Me and My Girl.* She wasn't concerned with her vowels. In just fifteen days she'll be onstage for *Sweeney*

Todd's dress rehearsal. Who is going to notice her Cockney accent if she can't even spit the lyrics out?

———

That Harry Katzman would play Pseudolus in *A Funny Thing Happened on the Way to the Forum* this summer had to be the worst-kept secret at Stagedoor Manor. He first caught wind of the casting two months ago, back home in South Carolina. Apparently one member of the camp's artistic staff let it slip in conversation with another camper, who let it slip to Harry a mere moment after promising not to.

"I've begged to play Pseudolus every year," Harry says. "It's been a running joke. But be careful what you wish for."

In *A Funny Thing Happened on the Way to the Forum*, Pseudolus is a self-important slave in ancient Rome, hoping to secure his freedom by helping his master's son find true love (even if it's with a courtesan from the house of Marcus Lycus). And it's been Harry's dream role ever since he saw the show at London's National Theatre in 2004. *Forum* is chock full of sexual innuendo, mistaken identities, and overheard (and often misinterpreted) dialogue; it's basically the *Three's Company* of musical theater. Sondheim based the show on the work of the Roman playwright Plautus. Where Aristophanes waxed on about the Gods, Plautus—so hot in 180 B.C.E.—was the original sitcom writer, the first to exploit the silly situations in which we mere mortals often find ourselves.

In *Forum*'s opening number, Pseudolus refers to himself in the third person. "Pseudolus is probably my favorite character in the piece," he says. "A role of enormous variety and nuance, and played by an actor of such, well, let me put it this way. [beat] I play the part." A smug, comedic role for a baritone? No wonder people have been telling Harry he was born to play Pseudolus since the first day he washed up at Stagedoor Manor, pompously handing out his artistic advice to directors twice his age.

Harry Katzman and a fellow camper, Matthew Meigs—co-stars in 2008's *The Mystery of Edwin Drood*—eat lunch with their cast. The display of lunchtime camaraderie, though heartfelt, was also a ploy to win the camp's Best Ensemble prize. Photo courtesy of Harry Katzman.

Ask Harry about his conduct as a first-year camper and he will now admit: "I tried to show off my knowledge too much. I was constantly trying to impress people. I was among my people for the first time!"

It has been quite a journey.

Harry is from South Carolina, by way of London, England. Listen closely to his speech—to words like *talk* and *hat*—and you'll hear a trace of the Blighty. Harry's parents, both Americans, met there in the late '70s and never left. At the time, his father was a psychoanalyst working overseas; his mother was traveling abroad, her life abruptly rewritten when she met this man. They married soon thereafter, and children—two girls and a Harry—followed like nesting dolls.

The Katzmans set up residence in Muswell Hill, and then Camden Town, a pocket in northwest London within minutes of the West End theater district. At the tender age of five, Harry saw his first show, a 1995 production of *A Little Night Music* starring Dame Judi Dench. This Sondheim musical—a soap operetta, really—is the story of an aging actress in pursuit of a now-married man she'd loved years earlier. Whether young Harry understood the machinations of these adulterous couplings or not is immaterial; at five years old, he fell in love with the theater. Two years later, the feeling was cemented at a West End production of *Guys & Dolls*. "I just remember the lights," Harry says. "It all made sense to me."

From then on, Harry practically lived at the National. "The theater was the one thing that calmed Harry," says his mother, Debbie Katzman. "He was catatonic."

At thirteen, Harry—a tad overweight, very expressive—sang with the well-regarded Finchley Children's Music Group, an audition-only choir launched in the 1950s by the well-known British composer Benjamin Britten. The choir performed all over Europe. They sang Bach's "St. Matthew's Passion" at London's Royal Festival Hall. "A lot of my friends had been in West End shows," Harry says. "Shows like *Chitty Chitty Bang Bang*. A bunch of my friends were up for Gavroche in *Les Mis*, but I was too tall to audition." He did, however, go out for *The Little Prince*, an operatic adaptation of the classic story that was being filmed for the BBC. While Harry didn't get that job, he made it past several rounds, and has since kept the letter inviting him to the callback. Ask Harry about his childhood in London and he'll tell you, with some hesitation: "I didn't think I was what people were looking for." For a kid who sometimes doubted himself, this letter from the casting committee of *A Little Prince* was concrete proof of self-worth. "Congratulations," it read at the top.

"Harry was very professional about rejection," his mother says.

"He'd say, 'That was a good experience.' Or 'Maybe next time.'" Of her child's sometimes shaky self-esteem, she says, "Harry's father was proud of him. But he never said it was good enough."

No matter what, Harry always had the theater. At age twelve, he saw *Jerry Springer: The Opera* at the National. He was a frequent visitor to the well-regarded Donmar Warehouse, where he caught a 2000 production of *Merrily We Roll Along*, a lesser-known Sondheim work that had closed on Broadway in 1981 after just sixteen performances. On weekends, Harry would often make his way to a music store called Dress Circle on Monmouth Street in Covent Garden. "In London," Harry says, "you're independent from a young age." The clerk behind the counter knew Harry not just by name but by taste, and he'd suggest cast albums new and old for the upstart maestro. "I'd use my pocket money for CDs," Harry says, and he accumulated more than three hundred cast albums in those years. Home at night, Harry would spend hours lost online, scrolling through the Sondheim forum Finishing the Chat (a clever nod to the song "Finishing the Hat" from *Sunday in the Park with George*). Needless to say, when it came time to prepare for his bar mitzvah, Harry was a conscientious student. "My rabbi used to be an opera singer," Harry says. "He was so excited to work with me. We had many more classes than we should have." At the party to celebrate his thirteenth year, Harry sang "Where E'er You Walk" by Handel—accompanied by a harpist.

And then his world fell apart. It happened quickly, Harry says. His parents separated. His mother later reconnected with her childhood sweetheart. And those dreaded words every child fears came: *We're moving.* Harry was suddenly forced to trade the freedom and thrill of the West End for the reserved swampland of Columbia, South Carolina. (At the time, Harry was so unfamiliar with United States terrain that for a moment he thought the family was moving to Manhattan—to Columbia University.) One of the last things Harry did before leaving London was to take the Tube to Southwark station, to the National Theatre archives, dragging his mother to watch a video recording of that Dame Judi Dench production of *A Little Night Music*, the one that started it all. For Harry, it seemed like a fitting way to say good-bye to all that he knew.

And then, America. In the fall of 2005, Harry enrolled at Heath-wood Hall, a private school in Columbia. "I was the Jewish kid from London at the Episcopal school," Harry says, summarizing his grand entrance. The culture shock was only compounded by the language barrier. He remembers taking an algebra test in ninth grade—his first semester on these shores—and making a computation error. Harry raised his hand, politely asking: "May I have a rubber?" The class broke into guffaws. Harry's math teacher addressed his new pupil. "Harry," he said in front of the class, "if you ask for a *rubber*, people will think you want a *condom*. What you need is an eraser." Ouch. (Harry's sisters were of some help in adjusting, but they had already graduated from high school and could only relate up to a point. Plus, Harry says, "They were the British girls in town. And they could drive.")

Surprisingly, even at a religious school in the deep South, it was the theater that helped Harry make inroads. In the spring of his fresh-man year, Harry was cast as Teen Angel in a school production of *Grease*. When it came to talent, he more than held his own, and the upperclassmen in the drama club soon adopted this outsized person-ality from Britain as their own. This association with the older kids conferred some measure of cool on Harry. Still, was he their friend, or some freshman curiosity? Even Harry will admit he wasn't quite him-self that year. "I tried to fit in with my idea of what a normal American teenager was," he says. But the only place he felt comfortable, truly, was up onstage. "There's no way to describe the high you get from being in front of a group of people," Harry says. "Not in a vain way. But you can give something back to them. And they can see something through you."

The academics at Heathwood Hall were rigorous, and the structure of the program certainly benefited Harry. But it was a small consolation. This was not an easy transition, and the anger was bigger than he could handle. "I threatened my mom that I was going to leave," Harry says. "That I was going to get on a plane and fly back to London." At the end of his freshman year, in secret, Harry applied to a private boarding school for the arts called Walnut Hill, located outside Boston. The tuition was something like $40,000 a year. He knew his parents couldn't afford it. He knew better than to even ask. It didn't matter. The application was more a wish than anything, as if simply sending that thought out into the universe was enough. It was a declaration of future independence, whenever that might arrive.

"Harry cried a lot that first year," his mother says. "It was awful." Of course she sympathized with her son, being marooned in a strange place. She was building a new life for herself, too, taking a job with the South Carolina Philharmonic to meet people before eventually launching her own communications agency, Unlimited Marketing Solutions. Harry, meanwhile, consoled himself with souvenirs. Harry's mother had kept every program from every show she'd seen in London. "I gave them to Harry," she says.

In these years, Harry clung tight to Stephen Sondheim's music, feeling a kinship with the characters in his shows. Those people onstage—the desperate Mrs. Lovett in *Sweeney Todd,* the lonely, love-starved Bobby in *Company*—were much worse off than Harry. "I related to Sondheim because everyone was having problems in his shows," Harry says. "It made my own life seem a little bit better." Harry read Meryle Secrest's biography of Sondheim and picked up on the parallels in their two worlds. In the book, Sondheim recalled falling in love with theater from a very young age, at a matinee of *Very Warm for May.* "The curtain went up and revealed a piano," Sondheim says. "A butler took a duster and brushed it up, tinkling the keys. I thought that was thrilling." Harry said much the same about seeing

Guys & Dolls at age seven. Sondheim's parents had also divorced, and as a boy he'd been dispatched to military school; Sondheim was as displaced there as Harry was now in South Carolina.

Perhaps to make amends, when the family moved to South Carolina, Harry's mother agreed to send her son to New York once a year to meet his grandmother for a weekend of theater. On one of those escapes, the pair crammed in *The Light in the Piazza* at Lincoln Center, *Sweeney Todd* with Patti LuPone, the new musical *Dirty Rotten Scoundrels*, and a still-in-previews off-Broadway show, *See What I Want to See*, playing at the Public Theater. *See What I Want to See* was written by another of Harry's favorite composers, Michael John LaChiusa, who happened to be in the audience that night. Harry cornered the artist after the show, blurting out: "You don't know me. My name is Harry Katzman and I'm a big fan of yours." For the next twenty or thirty minutes, the pair talked about musicals, about Sondheim. "You remind me of *me*," LaChiusa said. "How old *are* you?"

Yet even those weekends could be problematic. Returning home from New York, the cloud returned over Harry's face. "He'd had his freedom taken away," his mother says.

If Harry couldn't run away to private school and couldn't stay in Manhattan forever, there was a temporary salve in the offing. In the spring of his first year in South Carolina, Harry's mother asked her son what he'd like to do for the summer. "You can go to camp," she suggested. "That's what American children do." Harry googled "theater camp" and Stagedoor popped up on his screen. What's the longest one can stay? he wondered. Nine weeks? Okay, I'll do that.

In June 2006, Harry landed at Newark Airport and boarded the bus to Loch Sheldrake. His first role was Lazar Wolf in *Fiddler on the Roof*. The director, Raymond Zilberberg, organized a special Shabbat dinner for the cast; they sat in a private room off the cafeteria, eating challah and talking about what life might have been like for these hardworking peasants in *Fiddler*'s Anatevka. It was a transformative experience. Harry later participated in a workshop of *Rent,* produced in conjunction with Music Theatre International, the Manhattan-based firm that licenses shows to everyone from community theaters down to elementary schools. Reps from MTI were on hand for the performance. They wanted to see if a PG version of *Rent* (a show about AIDS and homosexuality set in New York's East Village) might still hold water. This was serious business. *Rent* composer Jonathan Larson famously died of an aortic aneurysm in 1996, on the morning that *Rent* was to premiere, and his parents (the protectors of his vision) traveled to Stagedoor for the workshop; MTI needed the Larsons' blessing to proceed with a version of *Rent* where lyrics like "mucho masturbation" were changed to "mucho medication." (They approved.) For Harry, that kind of immersion in theater was priceless. But the nine-week program was over almost before it began. For the final session that summer, Harry played the innkeeper Thénardier in

Harry Katzman as the crooked innkeeper Thénardier (alongside Rachel Geisler as his wife) in a 2006 production of *Les Misérables.* Less than 36 hours after taking his bow, Harry was back at school in South Carolina, and the abrupt transition was unsettling.

Les Misérables. He performed his last show on a Saturday evening, and thirty-six hours later he was back in math class at the Episcopal school. It was like being torn from the womb.

"In my mind," Harry says, "I was still in *Les Mis.*"

The theater can't be a substitute for life, though. And so Harry made friends at home in South Carolina. He lived in a bedroom above the garage. He would go to the prom. But if his high school experience could be summed up in a single anecdote, it'd be this: he was the kid who called his music teacher by her first name, and she let him, because it was Harry, and because she loved and respected him, too.

For three years, Stagedoor Manor was an escape, the long winters an unfortunate layover until Harry could return to Oz, Neverland, Hogwarts—pick your favorite childhood fantasy metaphor. The second summer, Harry's mother and her boyfriend, Rick, visited the camp, driving all the way from South Carolina to watch Harry play Judge Turpin in a production of *Sweeney Todd.* They were as out of place in Loch Sheldrake as Harry had been at home. Rick, a good ol' southern boy, asked a Stagedoor camper if he knew the score to some sports game that was going on that day. This little kid stared back at him in abject horror, saying: "Are you serious? Do you think anyone here knows about sports?"

Harry's mother was impressed with the camp. She could see the effect Stagedoor Manor had on her son, and would admit a different boy came home at the end of each summer. Harry was maturing— and not just in terms of his talent. Still, for Harry, convincing his mother to let him return was always a struggle. The camp was very expensive, and she pushed back. "There are other responsibilities in life," she says of her hesitation. "Like taking care of academics, like being a member of the family and the school community. And I never wanted him to peak too soon. I wanted him to have a childhood." (Harry's soon-to-be stepfather was so concerned the boy would skip college entirely, opting to move to Manhattan and start auditioning, that in 2009 he quietly called Konnie and requested she counsel Harry on the importance of education.)

In the four summers Harry has spent at Stagedoor, his mother has visited only once. "It's very far, and I own my own business," Debbie Katzman explains. In her stead, Harry's grandmother sometimes traveled to cheer on the boy. "And the other parents would adopt Harry," his mother says. "I was grateful for that. Parents always love Harry. I run into people in the bank here in South Carolina. They say, 'Are you Harry's mom?' I've gotten business because I'm Harry's mom." But in a camp where parents are often back and forth every three weeks—and the kids develop affectionate relationships with their friends' parents—it was an emotional divide for Harry. He simply wished he could have shown his mother off a bit more.

Like every challenge he faced, Harry turned the absence of his parents in the audience into a positive. "Some kids think, *My parents are coming so it has to be the best!*" Harry says. "I didn't have that. There was no one in particular that I was performing for. I was performing for myself. And for the entire audience." He thinks it through. "It was more about me performing for an *audience,* than for an audience that had my parents in it."

"It's almost as if Harry has succeeded despite me," his mother says, immediately recognizing how harsh that could sound. "I'm kidding. But I wasn't one of those—what do you call them?—helicopter moms. I wasn't hovering."

When it came time for Harry to plan the summer of 2009, his mother hoped her son would get a job. He'd already been accepted to college, and a damn fine one at that, the University of Michigan. So why return to Stagedoor? Harry and his mother argued. They shouted. And when his mom said she wouldn't pay for camp, Harry fired off an e-mail to Konnie: "Can I come?" A scholarship was arranged. And so, if Harry was working harder than everyone else on the first day of rehearsal for *A Funny Thing Happened on the Way to the Forum,* perhaps he had reason to be. He never once took his bed at Stagedoor for granted.

———

Seven or eight hours after the cast list was posted—setting camp in frantic motion—Harry Katzman stands in front of a mirror in a too-hot rehearsal studio in the camp's main building, sweating profusely. He is dressed in a striped polo, and when he uses the shirt to wipe the sweat from his brow, one can see a white undershirt beneath, tucked into his jeans, the cotton making a valiant effort to keep Harry's girth in check.

The director is slowly blocking (or staging) the show's opening number, "Comedy Tonight." It's impossible to underestimate the importance of this song to any production of *A Funny Thing Happened on the Way to the Forum*. While the 1962 Broadway premiere would go on to be the greatest commercial run of Sondheim's career, the show almost closed in previews in Washington, D.C. Why? Because of the opening number. In Washington, *Forum* began with a polite soft-shoe song called "Love Is in the Air." The problem: The show was meant to be a broad, slapstick farce, but no one had bothered to tell the audience. Thankfully, a new opening number, "Comedy Tonight," was swapped in, giving the audience permission to laugh, and *A Funny Thing Happened on the Way to the Forum* (which had once looked dead in the water) went on to run for 964 performances.

Today, the Stagedoor choreographer has a notebook full of suggestions for Harry. On the lyric *"something expensive,"* she wants him to wave his hand in the air, pointing to his fourth finger, as if he's wearing an expensive ring. Harry complies, wiggling his digits. On *"something appalling,"* she wants him to put his hand over his mouth in disgust. The director, Rob Scharlow—who once played Claude in a tour of *Hair* and is dressed as such today, wearing a tank top and cut-off cargo shorts—interjects with his own notes. He suggests Harry might want to go out into the audience and get a little playful with the crowd. Harry looks back at Rob, unsure if this is the right move for the character.

Rob: "Are you okay with going into the audience?"

Harry: [hesitating] "Yes."

Rob: "Are you sure?"

Harry: "Yes. Why?"

Rob: "Because you're looking at me funny."

Before dismissing the company, the choreographer asks the cast to run "Comedy Tonight" from the beginning, putting Harry through his paces. "You'll get tired of doing this one," the director says. "Because we're gonna work it and work it and work it."

Perhaps, but there's not a groan of displeasure at tonight's rehearsal. The kids are so eager to please. Yet, while there's been a lot of laughter in the room, that's not necessarily an indication of this production's potential. Everything is funny on the first day. The cast is thrilled to be there. The choreography is inspired. And the director's vision remains untainted, not yet threatened by compromises or by the ticking clock. Tonight everyone is too busy patting each other on the back to truly notice how uncomfortable Harry is.

But for this young actor, rest assured, the panic has already set in. Pseudolus has been his great wish, and he was intimately familiar with both the book and the music to *Forum*. He suspected where Nathan Lane had the score transposed for the 1996 Broadway revival; he knew the different inflections Lane used to distance himself from Zero Mostel, who originated the role on Broadway in 1962. Harry had begged for this part. But now that he was lacing up Pseudolus's Roman man-dals, he's not so sure. "There are so many expectations," he says, reaching for his ever-present bottle of water. "Everyone is saying, 'You'll be so funny! You were born to play this role! You *are* Pseudolus!'"

And just like that, the two-hour rehearsal is over.

——————

When Brian Muller spotted his name on the cast list for Sondheim's *Into the Woods*—he'd play the Baker—he felt as if this decision had been preordained. *Into the Woods* was the first show Brian saw at Stagedoor seven summers ago. That 2002 production—which would have been memorable anyway because it was the first to be staged in the camp's Elsie Theater, built to replace the Barn, which burned down the year before—also happened to feature an all-star cast. Erich Bergen (later one of Vegas's *Jersey Boys*) played Cinderella's Prince, Dana Steingold (the national tour of *The 25th Annual Putnam County Spelling Bee*) starred as the Witch, and Caitlin Van Zandt (Johnny Sack's daughter on *The Sopranos*) was the Baker's Wife. Brian and his father still talk about that production.

Into the Woods is often described as Sondheim's most accessible show, perhaps because the characters are familiar to any child. They include Little Red Ridinghood, Rapunzel, Cinderella, and Jack of the beanstalk fame—who hopes to trade his cow Milky White for cash so he can feed his worried mother. Sondheim ties the plot together with an original fairy tale about a Baker and his wife. A Witch has placed a curse on the Baker's house, and the young couple will remain barren unless they can deliver to her ugliness "the cow as white as milk, the cape as red as blood, the hair as yellow as corn, the slipper as pure as gold."

Act one follows this quest and ends like any nursery rhyme should: with everyone fat and happy. The first half of this show feels so conclusive, in fact, that when it opened on Broadway in 1987, Sondheim himself used to stand outside the theater at intermission chasing people down the street shouting, "It's not over!" The second act, well, that's the dark half. The show was inspired by the research of Bruno Bettelheim (a child psychologist who analyzed nursery rhymes for Freudian impulses). In act two, Little Red Ridinghood is reborn as a violent Lolita type. Jack's mother becomes drunk on their newfound (stolen) riches. And Cinderella's Prince is painted as a philanderer, running from his new wife straight into the arms of any woman he meets. "I was raised to be *charming*, not sincere," the Prince says (which surely qualifies as the best pickup line Sondheim ever wrote).

In a sea of self-absorbed caricatures, the role of the Baker—which Brian would play in 2009—stands in stark contrast. His is the most layered: the Baker both drives the plot and functions as the emotional center of the show. Cinderella? She talks to birds, and they talk back. The Baker, however, is on a different emotional plane. He's bullied by his wife, unsure of his life's work, unsure he even wants the baby she desires so desperately. There is a challenge here for Brian, even more so than handling the notoriously difficult rhythms of Sondheim's score. Brian is used to playing alpha males, typecasting even he admits. But the Baker is just the opposite. "The Baker isn't controlling the situation," Brian says. "That's harder to play."

It has been an unusually rainy week at Stagedoor—even by Catskill Mountains standards—and on the first truly glorious morning of the summer, Brian (dressed in red gym shorts, T-shirt, baseball cap cocked just so) and the cast of *Into the Woods* sit belowground in a windowless room off of the Oasis Theater, plodding through the show's twelve-minute prologue. (Belowground? If a kid doesn't have greasepaint in his veins, Stagedoor Manor is probably not the place for him.)

The prologue to *Into the Woods* is practically a play within a play, introducing each of the characters, and it's a tongue twister. To wit, the following is meant to be spoken and sung—in its entirety—in under thirty-five seconds. Set your watch:

NARRATOR
Once upon a time

CINDERELLA

I wish . . .

NARRATOR

in a far-off kingdom

CINDERELLA

More than anything . . .

NARRATOR

lived a fair maiden,

CINDERELLA

More than jewels . . .

NARRATOR

a sad young lad

JACK

I wish . . .

NARRATOR

and a childless baker

JACK

More than life . . .

CINDERELLA AND BAKER

I wish . . .

NARRATOR

with his wife.

JACK

More than anything . . .

CINDERELLA, BAKER, AND JACK

More than the moon . . .

BAKER'S WIFE

I wish . . .

CINDERELLA

The King is giving a Festival.

BAKER AND WIFE

More than life . . .

JACK

I wish . . .

CINDERELLA

I wish to go to the Festival.

BAKER AND WIFE

More than riches . . .

JACK

I wish my cow would give us some milk.

BAKER'S WIFE

More than anything . . .

CINDERELLA

And the Ball . . .

JACK

Please, pal . . .

BAKER

I wish we had a child.

BAKER'S WIFE

I want a child . . .

CINDERELLA

I wish to go to the Festival.

JACK

Squeeze, pal . . .

JACK

I wish you'd give us some milk or even cheese . . . I wish . . .

BAKER AND WIFE

I wish we might have a child. I wish . . .

CINDERELLA

I wish . . .

The melody repeats throughout the twelve minutes, but often with different inflections and different pacing. Brian stumbles over the rhythms, not to mention the accented syllables.

"The spell is on MY house," Brian sings. *"Only I can lift the SPELL. The spell is on MY house."*

The Baker's Wife argues: *"No, no, the spell is on OUR house. WE must lift the SPELL."*

The show's music director, Jamie Mablin, interrupts Brian. "It needs to be quicker," he says. Brian lets out a quiet huff, a rare hint of frustration. "That's the fun of Sondheim," Jamie responds. "It changes every time. That's why we rehearse."

Expectations for this production were off the charts. Brian was the de facto leader of what many people at Stagedoor had immediately identified as "the most stacked cast on camp." Katherine Lee Doherty, who starred in the original company of *Mary Poppins* on Broadway, would play Little Red Ridinghood. Charlotte Maltby, the talented daughter of Tony winner Richard Maltby, Jr., was cast as the Witch. Leah Fishbaugh (an enviable soprano with comic chops) would play the Baker's Wife.

Brian chose to deal with the pressure of these expectations in a unique way: by playing iPhone games during rehearsal instead of studying his lines.

"It wasn't just Brian," the director Chris Armbrister says. "He's lax. But I see that a lot from the kids who've been here before."

The Baker was the heartfelt core of the show, but as the first week went on, it was clear that Brian had not yet devoted much time to character study. Ask him about the Baker's motivation and he'd joke: "The Baker used to be a rock star, and the Baker's Wife was a groupie. Now he runs a special bakery—making pot brownies. But his wife backed him into a corner, and now he needs money."

Frankly, Brian is enjoying himself too much to worry. "I've done this before," Brian says, admitting as much. "I feel more confident playing a leadership role." After rehearsal one afternoon, the actor playing Cinderella's Prince comes to him for advice. This younger camper is having trouble finding the laughs in his scenes, and Brian is happy to help. "You're a prince," Brian told him. "Don't ever doubt what you say. Even if it's bullshit. You're the Prince! If you say it, it's now true." That slight adjustment worked wonders, and the kid was soon finding laughs where there'd only been yawns.

But when it comes to Brian's own work, he's less focused, and certainly not close to being off book (not close to having the dialogue memorized) for act one. For further proof of Brian's interest in good times this summer (as opposed to hard work), while Rachael Singer enrolled in Master Dance—an intensive, audition-only class that meets five days a week—Brian enlisted his friends to take a class called Master Modeling. Master Modeling culminates in a runway show for the entire camp. And in one of the first lessons, the teacher demonstrates the proper way to walk down the runway, stop, pose for the camera, and then walk back. Brian and his friends take turns doing the same.

When the class is over, Brian—who could be a wiseass when he wants to be—asks the teacher: "Will important modeling scouts be coming to the show?"

CHAPTER 4

Jack Romano

STAGEDOOR MANOR CAME TOGETHER QUICKLY, PERHAPS TOO quickly, for Carl Samuelson, who started recruiting customers in March 1976. Though Stagedoor's inaugural season was still three months away, Carl brazenly took out a newspaper advertisement announcing "Stagedoor Manor. Now in its second year!" Technically, this was true. Carl incorporated the business in late 1975.

"My father didn't think parents would send their kids to a first-year camp," explains his daughter Debra. Still, when Stagedoor opened in June, operating out of an old hotel in Windham, New York, enrollment was anemic.

There were other problems Carl couldn't predict. From the outset, he clashed with the tech staff, a skeleton crew recruited from the theater department at the State University of New York at Oswego, a team tasked with building scenery for thirty shows. "Carl bought us these cheap twenty-five-dollar homeowner circular saws," says Jeff Glave (who has since worked in production design on films like *Malcolm X* and *A Beautiful Mind*). "We'd burn up those saws within a day." Carl thought if he bought quality tools the tech staff would walk off with them. But his logic was fuzzy. Jeff: "We said, 'Carl, it's a *summer camp*. You know where we sleep!'"

"Carl always called himself a builder," Jeff says, and it's true, construction was his trade. "But it struck us that Carl was a builder who never built anything himself."

Though Stagedoor had been Carl's big idea, strangely enough it was his wife Elsie who fell hardest for the camp. On the very first night in Windham, Elsie was awake well past one in the morning, mesmerized as she watched the kids audition. She turned to Carl, who was expecting to commute back to New Rochelle with her at the end of the weekend, and announced: "Bring my clothes. I'm not leaving."

"It was like running away with the circus," says Debra, looking back on a time when her parents were suddenly the owners of a theater camp. "They had no idea what they were getting into." From the ashes of Berkshire Showcase—a mess of unpaid creditors, fire department raids, and a Ronald McDonald clown—Stagedoor Manor emerged. But what would make an otherwise sober businessman like Carl Samuelson invest in such a project?

"It was that crazy Cuban," Debra says.

—————

There would be no Stagedoor Manor without Jack Romano, the charismatic Cuban immigrant who served as the camp's first artistic director. His creative vision and educational ethos—unorthodox yet undeniably effective—influenced the early work of artists like Robert Downey, Jr., Jennifer Jason Leigh, Jon Cryer, and many others, and continues to be the basis of Stagedoor Manor's rigorous program.

But the man himself was a mystery. "No one knew why Jack Romano came to New York," says Jeanine Tesori, the Tony-winning composer of *Caroline, or Change,* who worked at Stagedoor Manor in the early '80s. "No one knew what he'd done, or why he was at camp."

That suited Jack just fine. He relished the mystique that surrounded him and was prone to telling stories. To some he claimed to have grown up extremely wealthy in Cuba. "He said his family had a pool shaped like a guitar," says the director Gordon Greenberg (*Happy Days: The Musical*). "And the house was a tourist attraction."

"Jack told me this story," says the playwright Jonathan Marc Sherman (whose drama *Things We Want* premiered off-Broadway in 2007). "When Jack was thirteen, his father took him to a brothel for his birthday. Jack told us in Cuba it was customary to get a *virgin* whore for your bar mitzvah. 'That's how it's done,' he said." Sherman was fairly certain this wasn't true. But the way Jack said it, you felt like it ought to be. And each supposedly true story was better than the one before. "Jack claimed to have won an Obie Award," says the playwright Nicky Silver (*Pterodactyls*). "I don't even think the Obies existed then! It would be like me saying I won a Blockbuster Award in the fifties."

There was no limit to his exaggerations. "When Jack's mother showed up one summer," says the casting director Mark Saks (TV's *Medium*), "we thought he'd hired an actress. She looked like an Hispanic Estelle Getty." And then there were the well-placed malapropisms. Jack would go to Burger King and order a "Whipper." Some actually suspected his thick Cuban accent was fake, just another theatrical embellishment. That he suffered from a series of mysterious ailments— a limp, an incessant cough—only added to the impression.

More curious, perhaps, was this man's temper. Jack—whose compact frame seemed much too small to accommodate his explosive energy—could be wildly inappropriate. He cursed at children. He threw chairs. "He threw a metal hanger in my direction," says Josh Charles (*Dead Poet's Society*, CBS's *The Good Wife*), who spent five summers at Stagedoor Manor in the '80s. No one was spared from Jack's outbursts. Jack's niece, Ana del Castillo—she wasn't *actually* his niece, but that's another story—appeared in Jack's *Evita* one summer. "I had this monologue," Ana says, "and I messed up my lines. Jack comes backstage during intermission and screams at me: 'Thank you for ruining my fucking show!'"

Carl knew little (or none) of this when, in the summer of 1975, he stumbled upon Jack's acting class on that fateful tour of Berkshire Showcase. Jack was addressing a small group of kids: "One thing that I really always want you to remember is that whenever you—the actor—is onstage, remember that the character that you're playing always *wants* something. *Always.* The moment you stop wanting, the audience stops being interested in that character."

Carl may not have had theater in his bones, but he understood this was no ordinary educator. "I found a fascinating director, a crazy character, a hypnotizing, mesmerizing teacher," Carl says in an unaired interview from *Stagedoor,* a 2004 documentary about the camp.

Jack Romano, a Cuban-born immigrant with a fiery disposition, was Stagedoor's first artistic director. In acting class, he often told the kids: *You have to be superhuman.*

"I walked into his class and I couldn't walk out. Again and again and again." With Berkshire Showcase in shambles, Carl invited Bob Brandon (Ronald McDonald) and Jack Romano to his home in New Rochelle to discuss how this all might work. In the end, Carl wouldn't assume any of Brandon's debt. (Nor would he work with someone who so brazenly misappropriated funds.) But Carl would happily take on that camp's lone asset: Jack Romano.

————

Jacob Behar Romano was born in Havana, Cuba, on July 1, 1937, the son of Turkish Jews who'd immigrated to Cuba. His father was a street merchant who sold clothing in town; his mother was a housewife. There was no guitar-shaped pool, no mansion in Santiago (another story he liked to tell the campers at Stagedoor Manor). Rather, Jack Romano grew up in a modest two-bedroom apartment on the second floor of a four-unit building, where he lived with his parents and his sister, Hilda.

From childhood, it was obvious that Jack was not like the other boys. "I was with him all the time as a little girl in Cuba," says Reina del Castillo, his neighbor from that era. "He made me laugh. He made me cry. I am a little bit different. I like art. I saw that in him. And I saw that his mother—she was screaming at him for nothing." In matters of parenting, Jack's father took a backseat. "His father was sitting in a rocking chair all the time," Reina says. "His mother was dominant. I think Jack left Cuba because of that. He wanted to, let's say, have the freedom to be himself."

In 1959, at the age of twenty-one, Jack flew to Europe to study acting at London's Royal Academy of Dramatic Art. At least that's what he told people. (The exclusive British drama school has no record of his attendance.) What is certain is that Jack traveled extensively overseas. And the timing was good. Back home, Cuba was in the midst of its own revolution; Jack reached his father, who advised him to stay abroad. Castro's macho Cuba was no place for a young gay man in the arts, he reasoned. And so Jack sought refuge in New York, working a series of clerical jobs to pay his bills, including a stint as a secretary for the Manhattan Shirt Company, a retailer based in Paterson, New Jersey. "Jack was bilingual and well read," says Jeffrey Zeiner, who once shared an apartment with Jack on West 21st Street. "He was good at typing. He had office skills." For a spell, Jack lived in Jersey with a boyfriend, and that man's mother. But when the relationship ended, Jack moved to Manhattan for a position at a travel agency, Fun in the Sun.

Like many gay men in those years, Jack took to the bathhouses. He loved the drama. He dated (among others) a police officer who used to pick Jack up at night in his cruiser. "Jack loved anything that sounded a little dangerous," Zeiner says. "He'd come home from the baths and say, 'Honey, are you awake?' I'd say, 'Yes, Jaclyn.' I called him Jaclyn. He'd come in and start squealing. 'Oh, he hung his uniform on the back of the door.'"

Jack began teaching acting classes out of his apartment, and in the mid-'60s he took a job directing children's theater at the Gateway Playhouse in Bellport, Long Island. That's where he met Zeiner (another director there). The Gateway kids gravitated to Jack immediately, Zeiner recalls. "Jack was extremely popular. His incredible passion was so sincere. And that accent!" When a kid did something impressive, Jack would clap his hands together and giggle. "He'd get so excited, he'd be on fire. And he'd light a fire under you." Through a connection at the Gateway Playhouse, Jack found himself at Beginners Showcase in New Hampshire, and then at Stagedoor Manor.

It was a strange and lawless time in the history of Stagedoor Manor. Carl moved the camp from Windham to the former Karmel Hotel in Loch Sheldrake, a sagging property that had been closed for five years.

Though the hotel was dank and musty, Carl recognized something essential in the place: it had space for theaters. The barn, the nightclub, the health club—all three could be converted into performance venues. "My dad was able to visualize it all," says Debra, now a lawyer in Manhattan. Carl bought the property out of foreclosure, signing the papers on May 3, 1977. With the aid of the U.S. government's Small Business Administration program, he took a loan of $105,000 from the Sullivan County National Bank.

Carl and Elsie lived on camp grounds, in a tiny yellow house that Elsie dubbed "Tara," an ironic nod to the palatial estate from *Gone With the Wind*. Jack continued to run the artistic program. Carl concerned himself with the business negotiations. And Elsie, meanwhile, saw to the safety of the children. She was tireless in this pursuit. Late into the night, she and Carl would put on their bathrobes and grab their flashlights, stalking the camp in search of children out past curfew. "Elsie

When Carl Samuelson purchased the Karmel Hotel, the resort's Club Oasis nightspot would be converted into Stagedoor's Playhouse Theater.

had radar like NORAD," says David Quinn, a camper from that era. He isn't exaggerating. One day early in the camp's tenure, Elsie went to lunch in town with a friend. At the time, Carl still believed athletics was a crucial part of any camping experience, and so he'd hired a tennis instructor to take these tiny actors off grounds for lessons. One afternoon this coach decided he'd had enough tennis, and if the Stagedoor kids could keep a secret, he'd let them loose for an hour in ShopRite. Unfortunately, Elsie happened to be doing a little shopping of her own that afternoon, and was understandably disturbed to find an eleven-year-old camper in the supermarket. "What are *you* doing here?" Elsie asked the young girl.

"Uh, we're at tennis?" the girl answered, sheepishly.

"Obviously you're not at tennis," Elsie replied. "You're in *frozen foods.*"

But Carl and Elsie couldn't be everywhere at once. Not even close. Excerpts from the extracurricular activities they missed:

As a camper, Jeff Sharp—who later produced the Oscar-winning film *Boys Don't Cry*—used to get drunk with the staff. "We would sneak out of camp," Sharp says, "and go to the bar at the end of the road." From time to time, he'd see Cookie Saposnick, the camp's first office manager, there, too. Here's how Cookie remembers nights at the local watering hole: "For one dollar you could get this mixed drink. It was six liquors. They called it the Colorado Motherfucker."

This was a time when teenage campers were actually having sex with staff members. For example, Shawn Levy, the director of the *Night at the Museum* franchise, remembers: "I was sixteen. And I dated the dance counselor. She was British and twenty-one. I'm not sure how much more I should say. I'm married now with three daughters. But it was crazy. Stagedoor was a bit like the Wild West. There was an anything-goes mentality." Well, not anything. Adam Pascal, who originated the role of Roger in *Rent* on Broadway, attended Stagedoor Manor one summer with a childhood friend, "who got involved with one of the male instructors in an inappropriate way," Pascal says. (That instructor was fired midsummer.)

Paula Lawson, Loch Sheldrake's first black camper (1977–81), recalls a wild display of drugs in the dorm. "I remember sitting across from four white kids and watching them drop acid," she says. "I'd never seen anything like that!" Paula came to Stagedoor from the Virgin Islands and it was culture shock for her, encountering these wealthy kids with bad habits and the disposable income to support them. Paula, who would play Ben Vereen's role in *Pippin* at Stagedoor, hung out with the kitchen staff after curfew. She was looking through an old photo album recently and came across a snapshot from one of those nights. "This kitchen staff guy was an Italian kid from the Bronx," she says. "And above his bed was a Confederate flag. A Confederate flag! It never dawned on me until years later what that meant."

Stagedoor Manor's kitchen was populated by wayward boys from a Bronx Big Brother program. But there were, believe it or not, *doctoral candidates* cleaning the toilets. True story: An ashram opened at the old Gilbert Hotel, three miles down the road from Stagedoor Manor. "People would come from all over the world to meet Swami Muktananda," says Cookie. The swami preached the joys of simple tasks to free your mind. "So the people who lived at the ashram got jobs as the maintenance crew at Stagedoor. There was an architect, a doctor, a plumber from Belgium—all cleaning toilets."

If Stagedoor was a circus—and no one disputes it was—Jack Romano was the ringleader. He was also the only reason kids returned to Loch Sheldrake in these years. Because the educational program he designed for the camp was game-changing, and worlds apart from your local after-school acting class.

The Stagedoor Manor ideology was *Learn by doing.* And more

often than not: *Learn by doing age-inappropriate material.* For a time, *Equus*, the story of a psychologically disturbed teenage boy who blinds horses, was a staple of the season. Likewise, Stagedoor was perhaps the only summer camp where fourteen-year-old girls regularly played Mama Rose, the sexually aggressive, control-freak stage mom in *Gypsy*. For a time, the camp actually used a scene from *Gypsy* for auditions. Girls would line up outside the playhouse, waiting to perform for Jack, each one muttering that memorable speech under her breath, "Nobody laughs at me, because I laugh first. At me. *Me* from Seattle. *Me* with no education. *Me* with no talent, as you've kept reminding me my whole life!"

You have to be superhuman, Jack would tell these kids. "He didn't want to see people grinning from ear to ear, belting their brains out with nothing behind it," says Michael Scheman, an early Stagedoor Manor camper. "He wanted you to dig deep." There was a difference between being an actor and being a performer, Jack would say. Scheman played Daddy Warbucks in *Annie* at Stagedoor Manor in the mid-'80s. "Jack and I went through the script, page by page, talking about Daddy Warbucks," Scheman says. "Warbucks was a Republican during the FDR administration, and what did that mean for him as a human being? And this was *Annie*! Jack didn't care if you were singing 'Put On a Happy Face,' he wanted you to find the truth in that character. And if the writer didn't supply it for you, you had to figure it out for yourself."

Jack could be unorthodox in his teachings, but rarely without purpose. Everything he did was in the service of the show. Casey Williams, now an actress in Los Angeles, explains. One summer she was cast in *The House of Bernarda Alba*, a 1945 Federico García Lorca play about an aging matriarch and her five daughters. Casey would play the sixty-year-old housekeeper, Poncia, while her best friend was cast as Bernarda, the titular mother who tortures Poncia. One afternoon, the two girls showed up to Jack's rehearsal—dressed in matching striped rugby shirts, as was the fashion of the day. Jack took one look at them and exploded. "You should have rehearsal skirts on!" he shouted. "You show me no respect!"

"Jack had a huge fit," Casey says. "And I ran out of the rehearsal because I didn't want to cry in front of him." For the next week, the girls barely looked at Jack, let alone exchanged pleasantries with him. Finally, Jack pulled Casey out of a dance class one afternoon to talk. "Casey," Jack said, "you've been hating me and cursing me under your breath all week."

"Yes," Casey said. "I have been."

"Well," Jack shouted, *"that's how Poncia feels about Bernarda!"*

"It was manipulative," Casey says. "But he saw us dressed as the Bobbsey Twins in our matching rugby shirts and thought, *How am I going to teach these girls?* It was effective!"

Jack had other questionable tools to draw out a performance.

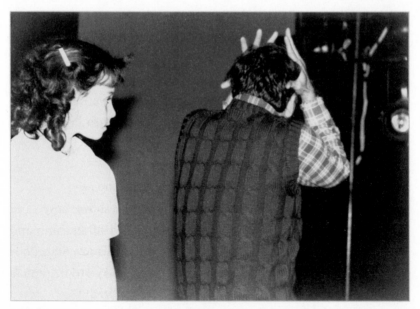

Jack Romano was known for his passionate teaching methods, always in the service of the show. He was also known to throw hangers, soda cans, and folding chairs at small children.

Every summer Jack directed *Jacques Brel Is Alive and Well and Living in Paris*, and it was an honor to be cast in these productions, even in a tiny role. One summer, while working with a female cast member on the song "My Death," Jack told this girl the song was about losing her virginity. Years later Casey Williams saw *Jacques Brel* off-Broadway. "You know what 'My Death' is about? Death! But death meant nothing to teenagers. So Jack told that girl the song was about losing her virginity, which was as close as we'd get to understanding death."

There were no boundaries—least of all when it came to Jack's improv exercises, which often included this setup: "You're in the anteroom of a Nazi gas chamber. Okay! You all know what is about to happen. PLACES. WARNING. CURTAIN." Jack would do that exercise with a six-year-old, says Keith Levenson, who worked at the camp in its earliest years. "He had no edit mode."

"Jack Romano didn't see age," explains the Tony-winning composer Jeanine Tesori (Broadway's *Shrek*). "He saw talent, or *not* talent. It didn't matter if you were eight or eighty-one. You were expected to work. And have that discipline." If a kid wanted to go to the bathroom in the middle of a rehearsal, Jack would train his deep brown eyes on the kid. "Your body only *thinks* it needs to go to the bathroom," he'd shout. "You can stand there for twelve *fucking* hours. Time is *your* problem! I'm the audience. The audience doesn't care about your *fucking* problems."

———

There's a larger point to be made here about these teenagers and their devotion to Jack Romano's particular brand of teaching and (by extension) to Stagedoor Manor itself. In its infancy, Stagedoor appealed to the same types of campers that had flocked to Beginners Showcase.

Jeff Blumenkrantz, who wrote the music to Broadway's *Urban*

Cowboy, explains. "One summer," he says, "this twelve-year-old girl at camp was obsessed with that Elton John album *Captain Fantastic*. I remember sitting around with her trying to figure out how we could stage this thing as theater—basically conceptualizing what we now call a jukebox musical. I was young for my class. I was a theater fag. I always felt *other than*. Let's put it this way: I used to *survive* the school year, and the reward was Stagedoor Manor." Suddenly he wasn't alone.

It wasn't just that these kids found each other at Stagedoor, and thus found a home. They found a *better* home. One whose rules made sense to them. Under Jack Romano's direction, Stagedoor Manor—unlike high school—was an absolute meritocracy. The most popular kids at Stagedoor were always the most talented kids. Period. The social hierarchy was constructed around a set of rules these public school rejects could understand: if you were a teenage boy and you could hit an A above middle C, or you were a girl and you could belt to a high E, you were a star. The cool table in the cafeteria was reserved for the truly talented campers—not the prettiest girls, or the ones whose parents made the most money. And that was liberating. At home on Long Island, David Quinn—a child actor who'd been on a season of *Sesame Street*, and who much, much later sold his business, Allrecipes.com, to Reader's Digest for a tidy sum—says, "I didn't fit in. One summer, this girl from my high school came to Stagedoor. My worlds were colliding! But for her, it was like the *Twilight Zone*. She couldn't figure it out. 'Why is David Quinn the most popular person here?'"

It's no surprise that musicals like *Runaways* (about teenagers on the streets of New York) and *The Me Nobody Knows* (about poverty-stricken children dreaming of "having a million dollars") were popular at Stagedoor, because they resonated with these campers—kids whose daily lives were so small, but whose dreams (as corny as that sounds) were so big they could only be expressed in song.

Ultimately what these kids wanted was someone to treat them and their hopes seriously. Because the emotions were that real for them, and the stakes even bigger.

Stagedoor was the ultimate parallel universe, and one of the first places a teenage boy could be an out homosexual. Michael Ian Black (*Wet Hot American Summer*) estimates that 80 percent of the boys at camp in his era were gay. And it was a nonissue. "It wasn't something people talked about over breakfast," he says. "I'm sure there were late-night circle jerks going on. I was there to hook up with girls. But the kids who were gay were obviously gay. They were pretty serious singers and dancers. And they also did the gay stuff that gay kids do." (Seth Herzog, a stand-up comedian featured on VH1's *Best Week Ever,* does a few minutes in his act about Stagedoor, pointing out the irony in the fact that the Stagedoor boys live together in one single dorm, and the female campers are forbidden from entering. "Who would care if the girls came in?" Herzog jokes, adding: "The counselors were gay. The choreographers, the directors, the teachers—they were all out. Basically, anyone who was allowed to touch us was gay.") It was a welcome reprieve from suburbia. This was Reagan's America, after all—that nihilistic time when the threat of nuclear war was in the air. A time when Harvey Fierstein publicly thanked his "lover" at the 1982 Tony Awards, and viewers were outraged! And yet here was Stagedoor—an oasis of freedom and expression.

"At Stagedoor, you'd have these teenagers, some of them not yet hitting puberty, walking around wearing leg warmers and holding a cigarette in their hand," says Adam Morenoff (now a New York City DJ better known as Mr. Blue). "Taking a drag on the cig and smashing it out with their Capezio. 'I'm never going to make my rehearsal.' Everyone bought into the fantasy of it all—that we were young adults learning how to deal with the stress of putting on a show. We were excited to get yelled at for not learning our lines."

It didn't matter how successful Jack was as a teacher because by 1981 (five years in), Carl was in the hole for $250,000. He was fifty-five years old—fast approaching retirement age—and he was forced to take a second mortgage on his home in New Rochelle, all to make this wacky little camp work. A camp where the artistic director threw full cans of Tab soda at young children, and insisted Carl pay to outfit the women in one of his casts with red press-on finger nails, despite the cost, despite the fact that the nails didn't add anything to the show, simply because that's how he'd envisioned the girls looking.

Enrollment was hovering around 150 campers per session—an improvement over the first years, certainly, but not enough to sustain the camp, at least not how Carl imagined it. Compounding matters, Carl was forced to offer scholarships to male campers. It wasn't yet socially acceptable to send your young boy to theater camp, but Jack couldn't exactly stage *West Side Story* without both Sharks and Jets. Meanwhile, to fill beds with paying customers, Carl oversaw the production of a promotional video, a sales tool he could send to prospective campers and their parents. Hoping to cast as wide a net as possible, Carl positioned Stagedoor Manor as an all-around camp experience that included swimming and horseback riding. On that first video, one can even see some campers playing softball. "That was the *staff!*" says Konnie, then the head of the camp's costume shop. "We couldn't even get the kids to play sports for the video!"

The camp had a profound effect on Elsie, it should be noted. "My sister and I were in our twenties when they started the camp," says Cindy who was living in St. Louis, working in marketing, supporting her husband while he went to law school. "Our mother was a housewife. And suddenly she had a whole new world. And these people were lively and funny and there was so much going on. She thrived on it."

Elsie would chastise the women in the office for gossiping about the staff—and then she'd charge in, insisting to know the latest. When Carl went to sleep, Elsie would stay up late playing Trivial Pursuit and Pictionary with Cookie, Jack, and another director, Michael Larsen.

But Carl and Elsie recognized they weren't the only ones with something to lose. To close the camp would have been to cut these kids off at the knees. (Where else could a kid be woken up to Jennifer Holliday? "Over the loudspeaker," says former camper Michael Scheman, "we'd wake up to the *Dreamgirls* soundtrack. You'd hear '*Bong. Bong. Bong. And I am telling you* . . . '") To keep the business afloat— to squeeze some fat from the land—Carl leased the property to the Sullivan County Community College one winter for use as dorms (until the undergrads trashed the place). Elsie, for her part, went on a fact-finding mission to French Woods, a well-known theater camp in Hancock, New York, to see first-hand why the competition was so profitable. Ron Schaefer, the owner of French Woods, toured Elsie around. And she wasn't impressed. "They served food on metal trays," Elsie said. "Like a prison!"

And then, disaster. Stagedoor Manor's finances nearly broke apart in the summer of 1981, when a wall near the camp's indoor pool cracked and Carl was slapped with a $7,000 repair bill. He was apoplectic. "We didn't know how we were going to come up with the money," Debra says.

"My father always said it took ten years to build a business," Cindy says. But the decade mark seemed to be further away than ever.

To save Stagedoor Manor, Carl would have to tap into the rich history of the Catskill Mountains.

For those unfamiliar with the golden age of the Borscht Belt, the Catskills was a bustling summertime resort area. Lillian Brown, owner of the nearly Brown's Hotel, used to brag to anyone who'd listen that she spent a million dollars a year on entertainment. And she probably did. Bob Hope, Sammy Davis, Jr., Liberace—they all performed at Brown's. And if Carl had his way, so too would the kids from Stagedoor Manor.

Troubled by the upside-down balance sheet at Stagedoor, Carl would often escape to the coffee shop at Brown's, where he struck up a friendship with the nightclub's emcee, Bernie Miller. Never one to miss an opportunity for exposure, Carl regaled Bernie with stories of the talented campers at Stagedoor Manor. Carl had a plan: if he could get his pint-sized stars up on the Brown's stage, perhaps the liver-spotted old-timers staying at the hotel would think, *Hey, my granddaughter should go to that camp!* Carl, a lover of big ideas, envisioned a touring cabaret of Stagedoor Manor kids as a regular act on the Borscht Belt circuit. Bernie seemed receptive. But then, nothing.

The summer of 1981 was nearly over, and Carl (strapped for cash) decided to force the issue. He piled two precocious campers—Gordon Greenberg (who'd already appeared on Broadway in *The Little Prince*) and Caroline Greenberg (no relation)—into the car and ambushed Bernie, whose office was so small the four of them couldn't all sit down at once. In the face of Carl's resolve, Bernie crumbled and finally offered up a time slot, sort of. "Bring the kids over tomorrow night," he said. "Lillian Brown doesn't stay up for the late show."

At eleven o'clock the next evening, well past bedtime, these two Stagedoor kids returned to the Brown's Hotel to sing their hearts out for the up-all-night crowd. "I don't remember what I sang," Gordon says now all these years later. "I just remember being upset that we performed in the small cabaret room, and not on the hotel's *glamorous* main stage."

B-list venue or not, it was a fortuitous evening. Murray Waxman, once a child actor of some renown, happened to be in the audience that night. He was responsible for booking acts for a hotel called the Aladdin. Perhaps catching a glimpse of his former self in these underage performers, Murray pulled Carl aside: "Can you give *me* a show?"

Rehearsals began immediately for a musical revue conceived by Jack, featuring songs like "If We Only Have Love," from *Jacques Brel Is Alive and Well and Living in Paris* and Sondheim's "Broadway Baby." Jeanine Tesori wrote an opening number for the revue—stitching together a medley of familiar snippets from *A Chorus Line, A Funny Thing Happened on the Way to the Forum, Cabaret,* and many others.

Jon Cryer was in that first hotel-bound troupe, which Jack christened the Our Time Cabaret (after a lyric in Sondheim's *Merrily We Roll Along*). "We performed in the bar at the Pines," Cryer says. "The crowd was eight or nine people watching TV and drinking. The cast vastly outnumbered these patrons who, God help them, just wanted to drink. They didn't ask for showtunes! But the management liked it so much they put us on the big stage a few weeks later."

Some parents would complain that Jack's troupe was elitist. And so Carl very happily expanded the program, creating cabarets of different skill levels. It wasn't as if those old-timers at the hotels knew the difference between the top-tier cabaret and the lesser talents anyway. In fact, Carl rarely turned down an opportunity to put the kids in front of an audience. He once took a gig at an Orthodox Jewish bungalow colony. "We had to borrow long-sleeve blouses and long skirts from the camp's costume shop," says Julie Stevens, who came to Stagedoor directly from the Broadway company of *Annie*.

"Carl sent us to perform at the Homowack Hotel," Michael Scheman says. "The *Homo*wack. You can only imagine the jokes."

Very quickly, Carl's ingenious plan to boost enrollment was in full bloom. "We performed at Brown's," Carl says, in an outtake from a documentary about the camp, beaming. "Sammy Davis, Jr., was in there on Saturday night. We were there Tuesday. And George Burns was in the following Saturday. One night, I had 180 kids out performing at the same time." And enrollment at Stagedoor Manor spiked. In 1981, some 229 kids passed through (staying four or eight weeks). In 1987, that number more than doubled to 490. Carl updated his signature advertisement in the back of the *New York Times Magazine,* (the place so many first discovered Stagedoor Manor) adding the sales pitch: "Our campers PERFORM AT MAJOR RESORT HOTELS."

Carl developed other schemes to improve the camp's finances. Namely, he tacked an extra week onto the summer. Previously, the camp season consisted of two distinct four-week sessions. But with a sudden demand for beds, Carl switched over to three, three-week sessions each summer. "That ninth week was all profit," explains Jason Teran, Stagedoor's camp director for seventeen summers, who helped Carl work out the logistics of the nine-week program. "You've already paid your staff. You've already paid for the grounds work and the upkeep. The ninth week is your gravy week."

In 1982, a four-week session cost $875. By 1986, the price for *three* weeks totaled $1,350. Beds were filling up. And Carl would stand in front of the cafeteria each morning watching the parade of campers pass by, welcoming each kid with his standard greeting: "Good morning, good morning, good morning, good morning, good morning."

And suddenly Stagedoor Manor was in the black.

If we are lucky in this life, we will each have one teacher like Jack Romano, one teacher who can open our eyes. "I grew up outside Washington," says Amy B. Harris (who wrote the famous "Post-it" episode of *Sex and the City*). "My parents were very cultural. We'd go to the Kennedy Center and see every play that came through. But Stagedoor is why I wanted to move to New York City—to be in a creative cultural environment. Stagedoor makes it possible. Like, *Oh, you can make a living at that.* You can make that your life's work."

Jonathan Marc Sherman had his first play staged during the camp's Festival Week, an early Stagedoor educational program where the kids would write and direct. So did Ivan Menchell, whose play *The Cemetery Club* opened on Broadway in 1990. (He now writes for the Jonas Brothers sitcom, *Jonas*.) The number of former campers who feel like they wouldn't be where they are now—wouldn't be in the city they're living in, in the profession they're working—if it hadn't been for Stagedoor Manor, is legion.

Jack never lost sight of the importance of the camp as a meritocracy. He wanted to be loved by all, but he was judicious with his praise. He would encourage a camper to see his talent through—but only if he believed the kid *had* talent. "Jack Romano took me aside after a workshop one day," says Michael Ian Black. "I had no relationship with him. I hadn't been in one of his shows. I don't remember exactly what he said, but it was something to the effect of *I think you have potential. I think you have something to contribute to this.* That was the first time in my life that anybody expressed that kind of belief in me. And it was overwhelming. Even talking about it now, it's an emotional moment for me. After that conversation, I wrote a rambling letter home to my mom, basically saying, 'This guy who is a demigod thinks I'm talented. And this feels like a first step to me. And I think I can do this.'"

It wasn't just the campers whose lives were set off in a different direction by Jack. Jeanine Tesori was a musical director at Stagedoor. When she wrote the introduction to the Our Time Cabaret, Jack threw the first draft back in her face. "*You* stage this!" he shouted. "I can't stage this." It was too complicated, not visual enough. It was more than just that one lesson. Jeanine had been a Barnard pre-med student at the time she came to camp and had given up on music. She landed at Stagedoor by chance, spotting a job listing in a binder at the student service center. She could have easily turned the page. Yet after one summer at Stagedoor, she returned to school and changed her major to music. "For me," Jeanine says, "Stagedoor was the first proof there was a chance of making a living in music. It had not occurred to me." This, from the Tony-winning composer of the ambitious *Caroline, or Change*—a show that transferred from the Public Theater to Broadway in 2004, not because any of the producers involved believed it would actually make money, but because they felt this important piece of theater simply *belonged* on Broadway.

Jeff Glave, who worked in the tech department for two summers, thinks back often on his time at Stagedoor. He built an industrial set for *Berlin to Broadway*—out of scrap metal he found at the garbage dump in Liberty, New York. He's a set designer still, and on jobs like HBO's *Bored to Death* or the Oscar-winning *A Beautiful Mind*, he's reminded of those early years working for Jack. "A film set is more like Stagedoor Manor than anything else," he says, "because it's a whole group of people, freezing outside with hideous jobs to do, but everyone keeps doing it because you don't want to let your buddies down. You want to come up with the best. We pulled a rabbit out of the hat enough times at Stagedoor. It gave us our legs, it taught us to be resourceful."

Yes, many campers from that era only spent three weeks at Stagedoor Manor. Is it the Royal Academy of Dramatic Art? No. But is it a valid learning experience? Absolutely. "You learn *how* to learn," says Jeff Blumenkrantz. "You can't quantify that. Even if you spend one afternoon with someone who inspires you—that's immeasurable."

―――

Jack Romano's fortunes rose with those of Stagedoor Manor. In the '80s, he traded his Hell's Kitchen walk-up for a one-bedroom apartment in the Sheffield, a tony building on West 57th Street. Jack was so proud of his new address, and the status it conferred, that he had a woodcut stamp made for all of his official correspondence. It read JACK ROMANO, THE SHEFFIELD, 322 WEST 57TH STREET. As a housewarming present, his longtime friend Irving Feldsott bought him an antique desk he'd coveted. And Jack, who perhaps never imagined he'd grow up, was suddenly playing an adult.

Jack was the pied piper—a self-created guru—and thanks to his winter acting classes in Manhattan, the good times never had to end. Jack was a firm believer in professional training (many of his exercises were borrowed from *Theater Games,* a book by the noted acting teacher Viola Spolin), but he believed equally in the importance of life lessons. At one point, his friend Emily West was dating Sylvain Sylvain of the famed punk band the New York Dolls. And Jack would take his fourteen-year-old acting students to CBGBs to see Sylvain play. "Jack had to show them what life was about," Sylvain remembers. "He said, 'You had to learn from experience, not from a textbook.' He was like Maria Callas. He was gorgeous like that."

It was a seminal time in these boys' lives. On Friday nights—from Long Island, from New Jersey, from wherever—they'd come to Jack's apartment and wouldn't leave until Sunday. After class, they might catch a movie or sneak into a Broadway show. "Imagine that you were living in the paradise of your teenage mind," says David Quinn. "There's no other way to conceive of it. If I said to you at fifteen, 'Go ahead and be the person you want to be and be treated as an adult,' wouldn't you?"

If Jack considered directing professionally in New York, he never expressed that ambition to friends. (However, he did live through a rite of passage for directors in 1980, when the *New York Times* critic Michiko Kakutani trashed a revue Jack directed at the Nat Horne Theater off-Broadway, writing: "The four characters . . . are gifted with good voices and good looks, but they are hampered by Jack Romano's self-conscious direction, which has the effect of posing them about the stage like mannequins.") "I'm sure if Jack had other opportunities, he would have taken them," says Peter Green. "But I never got the sense that, for him, working with kids was somehow less than."

And Jack certainly had enough distractions.

Jack moved his winter acting classes to the Sanford Meisner Studio on Eleventh Avenue and 23rd Street. He taught a fifteen-week session in the fall, and another in the spring, charging $600 per student. With seventy students each season, he was making $84,000 a year—in cash, plus whatever he was paid to be the artistic director of Stagedoor Manor (which was considerable). And Jack loved to spend money. On weekends, he'd disappear to Boston. "For sex!" his friend Irving Feldsott explains. There was talk Jack had a boyfriend, from the military no less, stationed in New England. "Jack flew back and forth on Eastern Airlines," Irv says. "He accumulated so many points he took me on a free trip to Buenos Aires for my sixtieth birthday." (Meanwhile, Jack told friends the trip was "research" for a production of *Evita* he would direct that summer.)

Jack embraced fine dining. "He'd tell the kids, 'Ketchup is like blood to me,'" says Michelle Federer (*Wicked*'s original Nessarose). "If you're going to sit at my table, you cannot have ketchup." He aspired to elegance. "He ruined me for life," says Michael Larsen, a director who worked at Stagedoor Manor for two decades and also taught with Jack in the winter. "We'd go to Gallagher's for steaks. We went to Curtain Up, which is now Esca. We went to see Angela Lansbury's last performance in *Sweeney Todd*. We saw Sandy Duncan in *Peter Pan*. We went to the closing night of *A Chorus Line*."

Jack lived on credit cards—a habit he developed late in life. In 1982, Mark Saks happened to be in London at the same time Jack was overseas recruiting staff for Stagedoor Manor. "Jack and I had dinner with my grandmother," Mark recalls. "And I paid. With a credit card. Jack said, 'Oh baby, you have a credit card?' I'm like, 'Yeah, I'm an adult now. I have a credit card.' He said, 'I don't have a credit card. I write checks.' And that inspired him to get every credit card they made. Macy's. Barneys. He had an Ann Taylor credit card! I said, 'Why do you have a *Barneys* credit card?' He said, 'I just have to have it.' He loved gadgets. He bought a photocopier. Jack called me one day. 'I bought a car!'"

In the late '80s, Mark Saks was in Los Angeles working in casting for Warner Bros. "Jack came to town with this beefy young actor," Mark says. "Jack called. 'I'm going to bring Tom to L.A. Could you meet with him?' I said, 'Okay. Where are you staying?' Jack said, 'The Bel-Air Bay Club.' That's where Elaine Stritch stays! Well, they were there for two nights. Then Jack calls me. 'We moved out. We didn't like that place. We're at the Beverly Hilton.' Two days later he called again. 'We're at the Ramada Inn on Hollywood Boulevard.' He was running out of money. I expected him to call back and say, 'We're at the Y.'" One time, Jack's mother came to visit from Cuba. It had taken thirty years for her to secure a tourist visa. "But he was ready for her to go at the end of the trip," Michael Larsen says. "She was buying appliances and washing machines for everyone in Havana—on his credit card."

Jack made money, but he was living beyond his means—oftentimes trying to keep up with his friend Irving who, like Jack, had champagne taste but also the old money to pay for it. (Irving's family was in the sporting goods business; the gun that Lee Harvey Oswald used to kill JFK was traced back to the Feldsott family distributorship.) Carl and Elsie used to refer to Irving as Broadway Irv. "We walked into Sardi's," Cindy recalls, "and Irv knew Gene Barry, who was playing the lead in *La Cage*. Irv had his own table at Petrossian."

Jack was prone to fits of jealousy, and as the camp's prestige grew, so too did Jack's résumé. Perhaps he was threatened by the education level and background of the younger staff, the up-and-coming directors who'd begun to flock to the now well-regarded camp. Or maybe he was just insecure. But when the *New York Times* sent a reporter to Loch Sheldrake in 1987 to do a piece on Stagedoor Manor, Jack suddenly identified himself as *Dr.* Jack Romano. The newspaper didn't specify exactly what Jack's doctorate was in, and with good reason: he didn't *have* a doctorate. At the same time, Jack liked to remind the campers of his past successes. Randy Harrison (Showtime's *Queer As Folk*) spent two summers at Stagedoor Manor in the late '80s. "Jack taught the best acting class," Randy recalls. "We did sense memory exercises, where we had to pretend we were waiting for the subway. The lip of the stage was the subway platform. Jack said, 'When a young Robert Downey, Jr., did this scene, he jumped off the stage right when the train was coming.' If only we'd thought of that!"

Jack Romano would brag about his previous students, including former campers like Robert Downey, Jr., pictured here in an early photo from Stagedoor Manor. Long before Downey, Jr. starred in *Iron Man* and *Sherlock Holmes*, he'd played Mr. Deusel in a late 1970s Stagedoor production of *The Diary of Anne Frank*.

But the party had to end sometime. Jack Romano's health was a topic of concern throughout his adult life. He had his first heart attack at thirty-four. He suffered often debilitating circulatory problems, and he ignored the advice of his doctors. He had gout. He limped. "You'd be walking with him and he'd lean on a pillar and say, 'Go ahead! I'll catch up,'" Michael Larsen recalls. Jack would get up in the middle of the night to go to the bathroom, and he'd light up a cigarette on the way. "He smoked with such conviction," Irv says, "which is how he did everything."

In the late '80s, Jack was diagnosed with lung cancer. Steven Chaikelson, now chair of Columbia University's School of the Arts Theatre Division, was helping Jack with his winter classes while Jack underwent chemotherapy. "I have a vivid memory of him being nauseous all the time, and on a couple of occasions running to the bathroom to vomit," Chaikelson says.

The Stagedoor campers understood Jack was sick—but only to a point. "Jack was *always* hunched over and coughing," says Michael Ian Black. "He looked sallow. I knew him as a chain-smoking Cuban. It didn't occur to me that he wasn't healthy. I mean, he was healthy enough to throw things and tell us what idiots we were."

True story: After catching a rehearsal of Zach Braff in a Stagedoor production of *Once Upon a Mattress*, Jack delivered this crushing critique in front of the entire cast, shouting at Zach and his co-star: "Did you two have a *lobotomy*?"

"I had to look up the word *lobotomy*," Zach says. "But I knew it was bad."

Michelle Federer remembers Jack trying to quit smoking: "Do you know how a Twizzler is hollow? In rehearsal, he'd cut both ends off and hold the Twizzler like a cigarette. He would suck air through— like he was taking a drag." Jack's health concerns were too troubling to be ignored anymore, and he was forced to cut back on his directorial duties. He still ran the camp's increasingly demanding artistic program, but only directed one show each summer. Naturally, it was always the last show of the summer—the J show, they called it—and rarely did it begin before midnight. It was a diva move. ("Jack was an egomaniac," says his protégé, Michael Larsen, smiling.) But Carl humored him, agreeing to the late-night curtain call. The third session had always been the toughest to fill. And suddenly there were campers who refused to come to Stagedoor for any session *but* third—just for the chance of being cast in one of Jack's musicals.

Jack had his detractors. But more often than not, they were campers he'd ignored in some way. "Jack had the best people in his shows," says Jon Cryer. "But he didn't cast me in one of his shows for the first two years. I took that personally. Finally he put me in *Working*. He said, 'Jon, I always wanted to have you in one of my shows!' I said, 'Well, Jack, you're in charge of casting. If you wanted me, you could well have had me.'"

Few held grudges, however. "Jack told me I was 'just a voice,'" says Jeff Blumenkrantz. "Later, he came to see me in *Into the Woods* on Broadway, and I remember thinking, *There! Just a voice, eh!*" Still, Jack's teaching stayed with Blumenkrantz. "From Jack, I learned about acting a song. I still use that—both for myself and when I teach classes. It's the ABCs. Here are the things you need to have considered before you get up and sing a song: Who are you singing to? What just happened? Why are you expressing this in this moment?"

"This memory will never leave me," says the playwright Jonathan Marc Sherman. "I was fourteen years old, rehearsing *Jacques Brel*. It was me, Jack Romano, an eleven-year-old girl, and the lighting designer—who was some stoned college kid working at the camp. Jack was screaming about the lights. 'It's all wrong! All wrong! I told you: I want it to look like a big red bloody vagina!' I remember thinking, I'm not sure I'm old enough to have heard that sentence. And I'm pretty sure *she's* not old enough to have heard that sentence. And in that moment I aged. I went through a growth spurt. My height was the same, but something expanded in my mind."

Sherman puts a fine point on Jack's legacy—the invented stories of a glamorous life in Cuba, the advanced degrees conjured out of thin air, the shouting at young children. "I think of Jack in parental terms," Sherman says. "You go from blind love to thinking, *Oh, you're just human.* You get a little dissatisfied. But by the time I was old enough to think, *Maybe half of what Jack said was bullshit,* it didn't matter. Because without him, I wouldn't have done any of that stuff I did. I guess if that's bullshit, bullshit works."

CHAPTER 5

Week Two

LUNCH. TUESDAY. WEEK TWO. 2009. LIGHTS UP ON THE
Garden Room—the exclusive dining area commandeered by the
camp's oldest, and most talented teenagers. If the temperature in here
seems a bit hotter today, if the smell is more pungent than usual, it has
nothing to do with hardscrabble rehearsals. It's something more ele-
mental. As in, the water. It's not working. For two days in the summer
of 2009, the main building at Stagedoor Manor—the one that houses
the cafeteria, all two hundred female campers, and the costume
shop—was without water. Considering that Stagedoor is the kind of
summer camp where even the boys might change outfits three times
a day, this drought comes with biblical consequences.

"This is like some social experiment," one teenager says, as if she'd
wandered into the Stanford Prison Experiment.

What happened? Well, the main building was aging, and a pipe
burst. While the maintenance staff worked through the night to rem-
edy the situation, the water had to be turned off. In the morning, a kid
would put a plastic cup up to the juice machine, and a drizzle of thick

syrup would come out. Cases of bottled water were brought in, and restocked frequently. Kids were brushing their teeth with Poland Spring. The tap was turned back on intermittently, with announcements made so the girls would know when to shower. Brian Muller and his friends, sensing an opportunity for laughs, took matters into their own hands, setting up a hose outside the boy's dorm (a building mercifully unaffected by the outage).

"We invited the girls over to shower on the lawn," Brian says, smiling. "We even put out shampoo bottles."

The stifling heat—coupled with the *Urinetown*-like scarcity of water—contributed to some already-building strife. Aaron Albert, who would leave camp to film his Disney XD series, *I'm in the Band*, in a few days, had perhaps the best perspective on the suddenly tense environment. "In the real world," Aaron says, "hot air rises. But Stagedoor is a bubble. The hot air hits the ceiling, comes back to the floor, rises again and gets hotter. It's theater camp. People are dramatic. I once heard a camper have a disagreement with a director over some part of a show. The girl was complaining. She was going on and on. Finally the director shouts, 'I have HIV!' How does a disagreement get to that point? Because Stagedoor is a bubble. And the hot air has nowhere to go."

———

Chances are, if you spotted Rachael Singer walking around camp that second week—between rehearsals for *Sweeney Todd* and her Master Dance class—she'd be muttering to herself. This wasn't method acting. She wasn't channeling Mrs. Lovett's insanity. Rather, Rachael was repeating bits of dialogue to herself, lyrics from the show recited out loud until she couldn't get them wrong. "I'm not a words person," she says over a lunch of ham cold cuts (her favorite). "I've just never had this much dialogue."

And so Rachael did what she always did; she took out her Hi-Liter and her headphones and she went to work. The Cockney accent had, in fact, been an issue for her. Luckily, the *Sweeney Todd* stage manager happened to be a charming Brit himself, and he was happy to sit with Rachael, dissecting vowel sounds and inflections as they pored over the script.

Rachael was making significant inroads. In a rare moment of free time, the show's music director, Justin Mendoza, offered to help Rachael with the pivotal song "A Little Priest," which closes act one. It's here that Mrs. Lovett hatches a plan to dispose of Sweeney Todd's victims. Standing over Signor Pirelli's dead body, she begins to outline the scheme, singing to Sweeney Todd: *"Seems a downright shame . . . Such nice plump frame wot's his name has . . . had . . . has!"*

"What does that mean?" Rachael asks the music director. *"Has, had, has?* Why does she say that?"

"She's thinking about her plan," Justin explains, answering the girl with a question: "What does Lovett want to do with the body?"

"Make pies," Rachael says.

"Right. She's going to use Pirelli's body for meat for the pies, right? She sings *has . . . had . . . has.* She's thinking out loud. Pirelli *has* a plump frame. But now he's dead. Oh, but wait! She can still use that body. *Has . . . had . . . HAS.* It's a good plan, then a great plan, then the *best* plan."

"The lightbulb goes off for Lovett," Justin adds.

And today for Rachael, too. She sings through the rest of the song with a new understanding, outlining the specifics of her plan to make use of the corpses. It begins:

Lovett: *"Seems an awful waste—I mean, with the price of meat what it is, when you get it, if you get it—"*

Sweeney: "Ah!"

Lovett: *"Good, you got it!"*

It was a breakthrough.

Rachael is improving hourly. By the second week, she's memorized most of act one. Her throat had been unusually dry, but she's taking care of that, employing a liquid product called Singer's Saving Grace, which comes in what looks like a nail polish bottle. "It's a saving grace!" she says. Rachael had gone for a costume fitting: She put on Mrs. Lovett's apron. She held the rolling pin in her hand, feeling its weight. And for the first time, she saw herself as Mrs. Lovett—even if she hated the character's orange wig. "I look like Annie," she says in the mirror, smiling to herself.

But at night, up late with her Hi-Liter, reading through the script, she admits there's maybe too much work left to be done. She's still rocky on act two, still dropping lines. But press her and she will admit there's a more immediate roadblock to her success. A more troublesome antagonist than Sondheim's score.

"I'm terrified of Natalie," Rachael says.

Ah, yes. Enter Natalie Walker.

There's an old joke in Hollywood, and it goes something like this: An exclusive party is under way on the night of the Academy Awards. It's so exclusive, in fact, that there's a VIP room within the VIP room. Believe it or not, in that second VIP room, there's yet *another* velvet rope. If you manage to get beyond that barrier, there's still another man with a clipboard. Get to the very last VIP room and just two people are inside: Jack Nicholson and God.

At Stagedoor Manor, get beyond that last velvet rope, and you'd find Natalie Walker sitting with God, giving him an earful about how *she* would have done the whole creation thing better, and in five days. It goes without saying: when the water at Stagedoor came back on for a brief time during the outage, Natalie showered first.

The thing is that Natalie Walker wasn't even supposed to be here this summer. She would start at New York University in the fall, and had planned on skipping her last eligible Stagedoor summer to go traveling with her boyfriend, who was finishing up his freshman year at Yale. "Wouldn't you rather go to Madrid with me than go back to camp?" he'd asked. Besides, hadn't Natalie gone out on a high note?

In Stagedoor Manor's 2008 production of *The Wild Party*, Natalie starred as Kate—a devious prostitute making a play for her best friend's man. Dressed in a red satin corset and black lace stockings, Natalie was *living* onstage. Andrew Lippa, the composer of *The Wild Party*, was in the audience that afternoon to witness Natalie's vocal pyrotechnics. (Tony winner Idina Menzel originated the role of Kate off-Broadway and killed it. But some might say Natalie possessed a more classically legit sound.) For Natalie, *The Wild Party* had been a star turn, and the culmination of four good years at Stagedoor Manor. But it wasn't a happy summer for her. Natalie and her boyfriend fought often. "And I wasn't really myself," Natalie admits. To make matters worse, shortly after she decided to skip 2009 at Stagedoor in favor of traveling in Europe, she and the Yalie broke up.

Natalie Walker played the jealous prostitute Kate in a 2008 mounting of *The Wild Party*, a musical about a cocaine-fueled 1920s affair. Stagedoor's production was the first officially licensed to a cast of high school students.

Panic set in two days before Stagedoor was to begin in June of 2009. Natalie logged on to Facebook. Brian, Rachael, Harry—everyone's status updates were all variations on the same theme, *Packing for Stagedoor!* It was clear: Natalie had made a colossal mistake. Thirty-six hours before the campers were due to arrive, Natalie sent a desperate e-mail to Konnie explaining that she'd had a change of heart, and *please please please* was there any way they'd make room for her?

And so there was Natalie, sitting in the cafeteria, in her big silver hoop earrings—each the size of an infant's skull. Of the jewelry, Natalie announces: "These are my bitch hoops."

There is a rumor going around camp that Natalie only speaks to people who are in the Our Time Cabaret. It's not true, of course, but the lie speaks to her status on grounds as a star. Auditions at the start of each session are done in pairs. But this time no one wants to stand next to Natalie. You couldn't blame these frightened souls. Who would *volunteer* to be compared to her?

It's not just Natalie's talent that is legendary at Stagedoor. (And it *is* legendary. One director describes her instincts as "flawless.") It's her eating habits, too. Like Elizabeth Báthory, the sixteenth-century Hungarian countess who drank the blood of virgins to maintain her dewy beauty, Natalie subsists on a singular diet as well: Pepperidge Farm Goldfish crackers. At eighteen—with her sharp angles and long brown hair, exuding a sexuality beyond her years—Natalie's metabolism is such that she can keep up her enviable figure by sampling from one food group: carbs. The way Natalie tells it, she wasn't always so hot. When she first came to Stagedoor four years ago, she says, "I had braces, bad highlights, and no one talked to me." She still jokes that her big break will be on NBC's *The Biggest Loser*—thereby joining the long line of preternaturally beautiful actresses who insist they're the ugly duckling.

Rachael and Natalie have been friends and roommates for years at

Stagedoor. And so when Rachael says that Natalie terrifies her, she doesn't mean the girl herself—but rather the *memory* of Natalie in a 2007 production of *Sweeney Todd*. Natalie played Mrs. Lovett that summer and her take on the role was different wholesale: where Rachael was silly and flirtatious in rehearsal, Natalie was sexually strong and calculating. She played Sweeney like Nintendo.

Of course, no one remembers the long hours Natalie put into the role. Or that she worked so hard that she alienated herself from her friends, who accused Natalie of being a snob. *Ever since you got Mrs. Lovett, you're too cool to hang out with us.* Actually, she'd just been locked away in her room studying the lyrics and Sondheim's

Natalie Walker (seen here with co-star Miles Jacoby) was a dazzling Mrs. Lovett in a 2007 production of *Sweeney Todd*—a performance much of the camp is still buzzing about.

syncopated rhythms, much in the same way Rachael was now. But no one remembers the sweat. What they remember was the result: Natalie's dazzling performance.

Not only was Rachael now struggling with the role of Mrs. Lovett, she also had to contend with the expectations of Natalie's delivery—so fresh in her friends' minds. If Rachael felt the pressure mounting, well, perhaps she was right to. "The buzz," one camper says, "is that this *Sweeney Todd* isn't as good as the one from '07."

Rachael had started to doubt herself, and worse, now feared others did, too. This feeling was familiar. When Rachael first came to Stagedoor four years ago, she was cast—out of the gate—as the lead in *Me and My Girl*. Landing that role was a coup for Rachael, an untested, new face at camp. But it came with an unexpected consequence, like when some of the more established campers froze her out. "I hadn't paid my dues," Rachael explains, with a shrug. That emotion—that her peers somehow felt she didn't deserve the role—was tough on her. And now, once again, that same fear was creeping back up in rehearsals for *Sweeney Todd*, at least in Rachael's mind, anyway. Actors can be their own worst enemy. At one point, Rachael went into Konnie's office to ask why she gave her this role. "Jeff cast you in this before you even came to camp!" Konnie told her. "We all know you can do this. You're ready!"

Natalie, meanwhile, who sometimes describes herself as "a gay man," is oblivious to the situation at hand and wanders into the *Sweeney Todd* rehearsal room one morning during a break from her own (she's playing Desirée Armfeldt in *A Little Night Music*). The *Sweeney Todd* score was laid out on the piano. Natalie, who'd taken to wearing chunky black eyeglasses—no prescription, just costume frames—glanced at the music for "The Worst Pies in London." "I remember how hard this was to learn," Natalie says, to no one in particular. And then she begins to sing the song—pitch perfect, in character, that textured voice of hers practically floating above the notes. *"Mind you, I can't hardly blame them—These are probably the worst pies in London. I know why nobody cares to take them—I should know, I make them."*

Slowly, one by one, the cast members wander over to the piano to listen. And Rachael, thumbing through her script, actually flinches— as if someone went to punch her.

———

And to think, Harry Katzman missed all of this.

The night before the pipe burst and the water supply went out from the main building, Harry stood on stage at the camp's open-air 150-seat Forum Theater running through "Comedy Tonight," the opening to *A Funny Thing Happened on the Way to the Forum,* the familiar strains wafting through the air. *"Something familiar, something peculiar, something for everyone a comedy tonight!"*

There's a moment in the song where Pseudolus, a Roman slave, is joined onstage by the Proteans, a troupe of foot soldiers, who serve as comic relief throughout the piece. "Only three," Pseudolus announces to the audience, "but they do the work of thirty." The Proteans, three young teenage boys, promptly stumble over each other. After disappearing offstage, these Roman clowns return with prop swords, generally making a ruckus. And from somewhere—it's unclear—a baby doll materializes on stage. The Proteans hold this Cabbage Patch Kid in the air, tormenting the plastic infant. Harry breaks up the scene, grabbing the baby from these clowns.

"Tragedy *tomorrow* . . ." he pronounces, caressing the doll fondly. *"Comedy* tonight!"

Stephen Sondheim's mentor, Oscar Hammerstein II, once told his protégé, "If the opening is right, you can read them the telephone book for forty-five minutes and they'll still enjoy the show." If so,

Harry was in good shape. "Comedy Tonight" was killing in rehearsal. The rest of act one was looking up, too. And so director Rob Scharlow pushes on.

In the next scene, Pseudolus is accused of petty robbery, and his master insists he return nine Roman coins to the man he's fleeced. Harry counts the coins out one by one, placing them in this man's hand: "One, two, three, four." Harry stops to complain: "I'm being cheated out of money I won fair and square!" When he continues counting, he skips ahead to "seven, eight."

"What happened to *five* and *six*?", the man asks.

"I'm *coming* to them . . ." Harry mutters, begrudgingly counting out: "Nine. [beat] Five, six."

For some young actors, rehearsal is a matter of the director pointing out how to get from stage left to stage right while speaking. But for Harry it's a chance to make choices, to throw a bunch of comedy against the wall and see what sticks. And Harry is growing comfortable with the role. Initially, he'd resisted stepping out into the audience, but he'd since found the humor in it. (For example, on a lyric like "something repulsive," he decided to point at some camper's weird uncle.) What the cast had was funny. But in terms of blocking—in terms of staging the show—Harry was keenly aware that they were running behind the camp's other productions. "We should have finished act one by now," Harry says. When he is reminded that the first performance is twelve days away, he responds: "Too real."

Harry wasn't being dramatic. He was legitimately concerned, and with good reason. Because he is about to leave Stagedoor Manor for an unheard of three nights, mid-rehearsal period.

On Sunday afternoon, at the end of week one, while the rest of the camp boarded the bus to the movies for a scheduled day off, Harry and his friend Chelsea Burris (in rehearsal to play God in *Children of Eden*, naturally) climbed into the backseat of a black sedan bound for Newark Airport. Harry and Chelsea were both due to enroll at the

University of Michigan in the fall. Unfortunately, that school's three-day orientation fell smack in the middle of Stagedoor Manor's first session. "Chelsea and I were really upset," Harry says. "Neither of us wanted to go. We were uncomfortable leaving our shows. We were uncomfortable with the place they were in." On the flight to Michigan, Harry did his part, studying the lyrics to "Pretty Little Picture," an act-one song where Pseudolus plays matchmaker to a pair of would-be lovers. But he was, admittedly, distracted from the task at hand. And who could blame him? He was off to meet the wildly talented class-mates he'd spend the next four years with. Leaving Stagedoor Manor for college orientation—much like leaving London four years ago—Harry once again felt he was caught between two worlds. "I feel guilty about going," he says.

For three days in Ann Arbor, Harry and Chelsea kept their distance, neither wanting to use the other as a social crutch. But when they'd drift back to each other—in the Michigan cafeteria, at a meeting—one would invariably say: "Where *are* we right now? What's Stagedoor?" Monday night passed, and then Tuesday night. While the water was intermittently out at camp, Harry and Chelsea toured the dorm at Michigan, picked classes for the fall, took their piano place-ment tests. They sat through educational theater. You know, skits about the dangers of drunk driving, skits about recognizing the signs of depression. Harry and his incoming musical theater classmates turned this into their own *Rocky Horror Picture Show*, shouting along with the proceedings. Between fits of laughter, Harry managed to turn around to glimpse the rest of his Michigan class—the engineers, the math majors. "They were asleep," Harry says. "But we"—the musical theater kids, he means—"were having such a good time." Which is to say, these were Harry's people.

The trip was a thrill on so many levels. Harry had been planning his escape from South Carolina since the day he stepped foot below the Mason-Dixon Line. (Harry meant no offense; some people are just built for a different climate.) Yet when it came time to apply to college, he fought with his mother. She'd asked that he not apply to Michigan at all. "You'll go where we can afford," she told him, asking him to consider a local arts school. Harry balked. When he was accepted to Michigan—overcoming insane admissions odds—he still remained only cautiously optimistic; he didn't let himself exhale until his financial aid package arrived and he was certain he and his family could swing it. In the end, Harry was awarded a partial merit-based scholarship, and he was genuinely floored by the idea. That feeling of self-doubt, that phrase that rang through his head years ago in London, had returned with a vengeance. "I thought scholarships were for pretty people," Harry says. "For tenors. For people who could play Marius in *Les Mis*." Would that feeling ever go away? What would he have to achieve, he wondered, to feel whole?

Harry had spent four years dreaming of college; his escape from purgatory was now penciled in. But at 3 P.M. on Wednesday, he and Chelsea returned to the Detroit airport and set off on the long journey back to summer camp. It was jarring, to say the least. "We'd been free," Harry says. "It was my first taste of college life. And now I'm going back to Stagedoor." Harry missed six rehearsals for *A Funny Thing Happened on the Way to the Forum*—a full three days of camp. If it doesn't sound like much, Harry clarifies: "Three days at Stagedoor is like two months in the real world."

Harry felt a momentary disconnect with his Stagedoor friends. It didn't help that he reentered Loch Sheldrake's orbit looking like he'd mugged the Michigan mascot. Harry walked into Barrymore dressed in a Michigan sweatshirt and a Michigan baseball hat—with his Michigan campus ID card swinging from (yes) a Michigan lanyard.

His Stagedoor friends had previously accused Harry of being elitist, of talking about Michigan too often that summer. So he tried not mentioning the trip at all. "I thought I was being respectful," Harry says. But his reserve only fed the fire. Harry's friends pushed him to share stories from the trip, and so he launched into tales of the fascinating people he'd just met. "Taylor Louderman is my soul mate," Harry announced. "She's so pretty."

Harry's Stagedoor friends didn't miss a beat, mocking him: "Oh, of course! You know *Taylor Louderman*! So fierce!" One couldn't blame them for putting up their guard. Harry was a walking reminder that their childhood was ending. That they were being evicted from Eden. And it was an awkward night at the boy's dorm.

Further compounding the problem, while Harry was playing freshman, *Forum*'s director missed nearly as many rehearsals himself, battling the flu. The cast still hadn't finished blocking act one. The work resumed. Harry had taken a step back. He was dropping lines, still using his script—not as a crutch, but for full paragraphs. Pseudolus is the show's rudder, and without his direction, the ship was listing. At least Harry was able to force a smile when one of the eleven-year-old kids at camp approached him in the cafeteria, inquiring about his Michigan orientation.

"Harry," the little tyke asked, "how was your *inauguration*?"

Harry grinned at the boy's mistake. "Well," he said, "it was *quite* grand."

———

Forget for a second just how challenging the score of *Into the Woods* is. Because, as if Brian Muller and his cast mates needed more complications, this show would be performed at Stagedoor in the round.

Working in the round is a distinct discipline, complete with its own difficulties. The show's director, Chris Armbrister, begins to block the piece, explaining the bumpy road that awaits these kids. In a standard proscenium stage, he says, an actor must be concerned with directions like *stage left* and *stage right*. But working in the round necessitates a different language. An actor must learn to think of the stage as a clock. You may enter at, say, number 9 and exit at number

12. Chris (dressed in a Hawaiian shirt with flames on it) likens blocking this show to "getting traffic patterns down." Adding insult to serious injury, you're also now acting in 360 degrees. "You're learning how your left shoulder should be lined up with the other person's left shoulder," Chris says, "so that you're not blocking each other."

Though the dress rehearsal for *Into the Woods* was fast approaching, though Brian had never worked in the round before, though he didn't yet know his music, he *still* didn't seem ruffled. If anything could be said in Brian's defense, the kid was at least inspired by the music of *Into the Woods*. Though perhaps not in the way Konnie had imagined when she cast him as the Baker.

It is the middle of week two, and the Camper Showcase is upon us. In an effort to let younger, newer talent on camp shine, spots in this evening's talent show—held in the Playhouse Theater—are off limits to the more established Stagedoor names, namely the members of the Our Time Cabaret. Rather, the Camper Showcase is a chance for the next generation of all-stars to show off. What's so thrilling about tonight is the surprises. A supporting player from *Sweeney Todd* sings "It Sucks to Be Me" from *Avenue Q*, and—amazingly and convincingly—he does all seven different character voices himself. (From backstage, the performance is nearly indistinguishable from the original Broadway recording.) Then a shy teenage girl so painfully awkward she probably wouldn't look you in the eye as she was shaking your hand, sits herself down in front of the piano and performs a pop cover, "Almost Lover." *"Good-bye, my almost lover,"* she sings, hauntingly, *"good-bye, my hopeless dream. I'm trying not to think about you."*

And then there's Brian. It's become a rite of passage for a select group of older kids to host the Camper Showcase—a job not unlike hosting any awards show. One must write an opening sketch, plus comic interludes between the acts. Tonight, Brian, Natalie, and two of their friends handle the duties. For the opening skit, Brian hit upon the idea of adapting the prologue from *Into the Woods*, transporting the action from the forest to the halls of Stagedoor Manor. Rather than the song telling the story of Cinderella, Jack, and the Baker, Brian and his friends would recast the lyrics to introduce four Stagedoor archetypes: The dim athlete who couldn't sing, the frustrated hot single girl amidst a sea of gay men, the confused boy wrestling with his sexuality (while trying to squeeze into a pair of tight-fitting jean shorts), and the tech camper coming to Stagedoor to apprentice in set design. (Tech campers are an urban legend; no one has any proof they really exist.)

The night before Camper Showcase, Brian and his friends collaborated on the lyrics to this opening sketch, staying up well past curfew, which explains why Brian doesn't yet know his lines for *Into the Woods*. Still, judging by the audience response, it was time well spent.

In the original prologue to *Into the Woods*, Jack begs his cow to offer up a few drops of milk, singing *"Please pal . . . squeeze pal."* In Brian's comic version, the sexually confused character stands onstage singing: *"Please jorts, squeeze jorts."* Where the Baker sings, *"I wish we had a child. I want a child,"* tonight Natalie belts: *"I wish I had a guy. A straight guy!"* The laughter drowns out much of what comes next.

Was the skit Sondheim? No. Was it clever? Undeniably. More important, was it Stagedoor? To the bone.

———

Brian was pleased with himself and his hosting prowess at the Camper Showcase. How could he not be? But at rehearsal the next day, his lax attitude toward this summer finally caught up with him.

The director of *Into the Woods*, Chris Armbrister, asks to run the prologue again. Brian takes his place, at number 6 on the clock, alongside the Baker's Wife. He is preparing to head into the woods in search of the four items the Witch demanded—the four items that will break the curse and deliver them a child. *"The spell is on MY house,"* Brian sings, throwing his red knapsack over his shoulder like a fashion model and posing in tableau.

The director interrupts. "It's not a JCPenney ad," he says to Brian, eliciting a laugh from the cast.

If the sharp critique—insightful and spot on—hit home with Brian, perhaps it's because he'd heard something similar before.

Brian came to Stagedoor Manor on a lark eight years ago. When camp ends this summer, he will take a few weeks off before beginning rehearsals for the national tour of *Little House on the Prairie*—his first professional credit, his first Equity tour. Brian's mother still isn't sure when her son's acting went from a hobby to a career, or to put it another way, from one Tostitos audition at age thirteen to a life plan.

Brian Muller participated in a workshop of *Avenue Q* at Stagedoor Manor in 2005. Jeff Whitty, the Tony-winning book writer for the show, traveled to Loch Sheldrake to advise the young cast.

Brian, however, remembers the precise moment that seed was planted. And refreshingly, it wasn't when he got an agent. Or cashed his first paycheck. Rather, he made the decision independently, with all the thought and care a choice like that merits. In 2005, Brian was cast in a Stagedoor production of *Our Town*. The show's director, Michael Raimondi, was teaching the camp's Master Acting class that session, and Brian enrolled. In class one afternoon, the teacher went around the room asking each camper a different highly personal question. It was awkward, it was challenging—it was all of the things a serious acting class should be. And then the teacher turned to Brian and, in front of his young peers, he zeroed in on a tic in this boy's personality. "Brian," he asked. "Do you know when you're bullshitting?"

That tendency to slide by on charm when introspection was called for, to crack wise in serious situations, the teacher recognized that in Brian. And he wanted to scratch beneath the surface to see if there was anything there worth mining. "Do you know when you're bullshitting?" this man repeated. ("It's not a JCPenney ad," he might as well have said.)

"Yes," Brian insisted. He *did* know.

And from that moment on, Brian worked differently—harder, but also smarter and with intention. In *Our Town*, Brian had been cast as George Gibbs, the doctor's son, and he tore through the pages. "It was one of the first times I looked at a script and thought, *Why is my character saying this here?*" Brian says. "*What am I thinking here?* I wasn't just memorizing a monologue. I wasn't just getting through it." The work showed. Finally, there was something behind Brian's eyes onstage. He wasn't just a cute kid. There is a scene in act three of *Our Town* where George kneels over his wife's grave; she's just died giving birth to their child. The scene was staged during an evening rehearsal on Stagedoor's front lawn. "It was dark," Brian says. "I got down on my knees and I started hugging the ground and crying." Brian caught even himself by surprise. "That was the first time I'd had an emotion like that onstage."

After the rehearsal, Brian spoke with the director, looking to share the breakthrough with him. "If I'm crying like this during rehearsal," Brian said, proudly, "I'll be a mess during the show!"

The director stared back at Brian and offered some advice. "Don't talk about it," he said. "Don't talk about what happened tonight. Because if you do, it's gonna lose its meaning. And by the time you get to the performance, you won't be able to cry."

"Sure enough," Brian says now, looking back on the formative experience, "I didn't cry from that point on—because I thought about it too much." In high school, an acting teacher later broached this same concept. He called it *leaking*. Every time you tell someone about a moment, you are giving part of it away. The thought stuck with Brian, who'd come to see acting as a craft. During Brian's junior year of high school, a teacher asked him why he wanted to go to college. He didn't hesitate: "I want to learn to be an actor."

It was decided. This would be his future. "I feel different when I'm onstage," Brian says. "It's hard to explain." Yet that's enough.

In some ways, that idea of giving it away—what the teacher called *leaking*—had become part of Brian's persona. When he got the job in *Little House on the Prairie* tour—in a cast with Melissa Gilbert, directed by Francesca Zambello—Brian kept the news to himself. He told very few people personally. "I've been in situations where people start a conversation," Brian says, "and the entire basis of the conversation is so they can tell you about their success. Like, 'Hey, how are you?' And before you can answer they say, 'Guess what, I got this job!'" He didn't want to be that guy.

Two weeks into the summer of 2009, after that rehearsal for *Into the Woods*—in which he didn't know his lines, didn't know much more than the traffic patterns—Brian didn't make some big pronouncement about committing himself to the show, or some big phony speech. Instead he opened up the script and started asking questions. Who *was* the Baker? Why was this character so unsure of his future? Did he really want to have a child, or was he merely placating his wife?

A flubbed line here or there didn't get under his skin. "I'm fine not being spot-perfect," Brian says. "As long as I can still gain something from rehearsal. But I didn't know the script well enough to be productive." And so back in his dorm room—consisting of a few bunk beds and a bathroom he shared with Harry Katzman and three other campers—Brian now stayed up well past curfew, borrowing a flashlight to study his script. He put in his headphones and listened to *Into the Woods*, rewinding to go over the rhythms, the accents, the lyrics, the pauses.

And the next day Brian Muller showed up at rehearsal ready to work.

CHAPTER 6

Carl and Elsie

ON MARCH 21, 1991, JACK ROMANO COLLAPSED IN THE LOBBY of the Sheffield on West 57th Street. He'd suffered a heart attack and was rushed to St. Luke's Hospital where he was pronounced dead. He was fifty-three years old.

Carl and Elsie Samuelson began the funeral arrangements, and joined Debra, David Quinn, Michael Larsen—some of Jack's closest friends from Stagedoor Manor—in cleaning out his apartment. They found tickets for upcoming shows. "We found clothing he never wore," Larsen says. "Shoes he never wore."

"He spent everything," says David, still teary-eyed almost two decades later. "That's how he lived."

Jack's funeral was held at Riverside Memorial Chapel on Amsterdam and 76th on Sunday, March 24, 1991, and it was standing room only. "It was like the end of *Mr. Holland's Opus*," says Michael Ian Black. "The place was full of these people whose lives you knew he'd touched." They came for many reasons, but mostly because without Jack, who knows where they'd be?

No one suffered any delusions that Jack's passing was a minor event. "I cried often that summer," says Konnie, who was later promoted from the costume shop to the title of Stagedoor's production director. "I said, 'Jack, Why did you leave me? I can't do what you did. I can't get those performances out of those kids.'" In the wake of this untimely loss, Jack's final show, *Man of La Mancha*, took on mythic proportions. That production starred a young Danny Gurwin (Broadway's *Little Women*) as Don Quixote and Michelle Federer (*Wicked*) as Aldonza, and Jack's backstage histrionics were extreme—even by his own perverted standards; it was as if Jack knew this would be his final show. During rehearsals, Jack now-famously asked the stage manager if she could procure a live dove—a dove!—for Quixote to hold while singing "The Impossible Dream."

"I want it to look like he's been communing with nature," Jack shouted.

A second memorial was organized for July 28, 1991, at the Raleigh Hotel in South Fallsberg. The quintet from Jack's last *West Side Story* performed (a cast that included Broadway's Julia Murney as Anita). The guests joined together to sing Jack's favorite song, "If We Only Have Love," from *Jacques Brel Is Alive and Well and Living in Paris*. Back at camp, hundreds of black helium balloons were released into the air. And, in a short ceremony, Carl renamed the Playhouse Theater in Jack's honor. In the lobby of the newly christened Jack Romano Playhouse, Carl hung a framed black-and-white photo of Jack alongside these lyrics from Sondheim's *Merrily We Roll Along*: "*Years from now, we'll remember and we'll come back . . . This is where we began, being what we can.*" For three years after Jack's death the maintenance crew would have to wipe that very frame clean daily. Because the kids—heartbroken, still reeling—would kiss Jack's photo, leaving streak marks all over the glass.

For pop culture historians, the '90s didn't begin until September 24, 1991—the day Nirvana's *Nevermind* was released. At Stagedoor, it was March 21, 1991, the day they lost Jack Romano.

It's almost poetic that Jack Romano died in 1991. The sea change was that sharp. Throwing chairs? Cursing at students? Behavior like that passed muster in the '70s but was certainly out of fashion by the time of his passing. "I don't want to admit it was another era, but it was," says Jack's protégé, Michael Larsen, who worked at Stagedoor for twenty-four years. "We made our kids hyperaware of the bad things that adults can do to them. Which is good and bad. There's that old joke among teachers, 'You gotta bring a lawyer with you to work.' You need five witnesses to pat a kid on the back and say, 'Job well done.'" Perhaps it was better that Jack never had to compromise.

In many ways, Michael filled the role vacated by Jack. He was the defining teacher of that next decade. "Michael Larsen was everything to us," says Drew Elliott, now the vice president of marketing for the downtown Manhattan magazine, *Paper*. Larsen attempted to keep Jack's stricture alive. And he could be just as unorthodox. When Michael directed a production of *Hair* one summer, the show actually began outside the theater. Parents watched the cast of make-believe hippies roll around on the grass, kissing and hugging each other, before they skipped over to the theater to begin the show. Todd Buonopane (who later starred in *The 25th Annual Putnam County Spelling Bee* on Broadway) was in a production of *Applause* that Michael directed. "He was shouting at me, 'Pick up your cues! Pick up your cues! You're losing people!' I wasn't talking fast enough. In front of everyone, he said to the stage manager, 'Give me the cast list! I need to pick someone from the chorus to replace Todd.'"

"I still think about that in rehearsal even now," Todd says. "Why are people speaking so slowly? Spit it out!"

But in the wake of Jack's death, Carl and Elsie became the dominant personalities. And that had profound effects on Stagedoor Manor.

"We were discouraged from pushing the kids too hard," Michael says. Carl was getting older, and he had less patience for these theatrical personalities—especially since the camp was making money hand over (bedazzled) fist. The Our Time Cabaret continued touring the area hotels under Michael's direction, and the young girls on campus were so eager to please him that they'd stay up way past curfew rehearsing their harmonies in the stairwells. "We'd have arguments in the office about the kids staying up so late," says Ellen Kleiner, who continues to work at Stagedoor. "Carl wanted the kids to go to bed."

Carl could afford to push back. If Jack Romano had been the selling point for the first fifteen years of Stagedoor Manor's history—and some campers from that era express outright shock that the place could possibly carry on without him—Carl had a different pitch now.

In 1984, a former camper, Todd Graff, received a Tony Award

Carl Samuelson behind his desk in Stagedoor Manor's main office. Carl would often come out to greet the children on their way into breakfast, famously repeating this phrase: "Good morning, good morning, good morning, good morning, good morning."

nomination for *Baby* on Broadway. That same year, Helen Slater—another alum—was cast in the title role of the big-screen *Supergirl*, opposite Faye Dunaway. Robert Downey, Jr. was starring in *Back to School* and *Less than Zero*. Jennifer Jason Leigh. Mary Stuart Masterson. In profiles and publicity, these names were linked to that funny theater camp in, of all places, Loch Sheldrake, New York. As Stagedoor Manor's profile rose, casting directors and talent managers started making the trek upstate. "I used to call the camp a gold mine of talent," says Jean Fox, who managed young actors through her firm Fox/Albert and often scouted at Stagedoor. An August 6, 1987, segment on CNN's *Showbiz Today* had presaged a new era. "We have no flagpole," Carl says in the TV piece. "Our camp song is all the songs that have ever been written for Broadway. And we have 250 fabulously talented kids. Kids who love theater." The camera cuts to David John, a young tyke about to depart Loch Sheldrake. Why? "I got a part in *Les Misérables*," he says. On Broadway.

Seth Herzog (a comedian who now warms up Jimmy Fallon's studio audience nightly) puts a fine point on it: "Jon Cryer left camp to do *Brighton Beach* on Broadway. And then he did *No Small Affair*, the Demi Moore movie. He went from the guy in my bunk to being a film star. Scott Schustman—who went by Scott Tyler—left camp in the middle of the summer to do *Once Upon a Time in America*. He played the young Bobby De Niro part. There was this vibe: This is happening."

Carl, sniffing yet another marketing tool, compiled a list of every camper who was cashing a paycheck—in theater, in film, in television commercials—and that list was mailed out to prospective campers and their parents. If anybody did something of note, it was included in that letter. It started as a skinny packet. And then it wasn't. The message: Stagedoor Manor might be more expensive than other summer camps, but the tuition is nothing short of an investment in your child's future.

And for the first time, talented suburban children with no connections to show business could see a through line to Hollywood. In the '90s, the big opportunities for child actors were *The Mickey Mouse Club* and *Kids Incorporated*—both run out of Orlando, Florida. "If you wanted to be discovered," says Marshall Heyman (now a journalist covering Hollywood for glossy publications like *W* magazine), "you went to Orlando. But our parents weren't moving us to Orlando. There weren't any Disney Channel sitcoms. And even if there were, our parents wouldn't have wanted us to be on one. We went to auditions for game shows like *Steampipe Alley* and *Kids Court*." No one expected to be discovered scooping ice cream at Cold Stone Creamery—as Long Island's Nikki Blonsky later would be for the movie *Hairspray*. Unsure of what to do, parents sent their kids to Stagedoor.

This dovetailed nicely with a change in the nation's attitude toward summer camps, which (as an institution) had previously been about little more than nature hikes and canoe trips—not to mention an eight-week reprieve for weary parents. But the 1990s saw a boom in specialty camps across the United States, from wildly expensive athletic programs to NASA-sponsored space camps. "Previously, kids would go to the same camp year after year," says Peg Smith, the CEO of the American Camp Association. "But kids started to collect a menu of experiences—they'd go to soccer camp for three weeks, then music camp for three weeks, and then a traditional camp for three weeks." The number of specialty camps in these years exploded— you no longer had to send your kid to a theater camp run by a drunk Ronald McDonald clown. Parents were now employing professional camp advisors, in the same way they might enlist a college counselor to guide them through the labyrinthine university application process. These parents now came armed with questions: they wanted to know about staff-to-camper ratios, retention rates, and other quantitative metrics of a camp's success. Carl had all the right answers. And whether you were serious about acting professionally, or just serious about that immersive experience of theater-as-oxygen for a summer, Stagedoor was the name on everyone's lips. "If you wanted to act," Marshall says, "you went to Stagedoor. Everyone was cast in a show."

Stagedoor Manor took on a surreal quality in these years, as Carl became something of the Broadway Danny Rose of theater camp owners. "Carl would call me and say, 'You have to meet this twelve-year-old girl. She's incredible!'" says Nancy Carson, a well-known New York talent agent who regularly scouts at Stagedoor Manor. "I'd say okay. And this girl would come into my office. And she'd be terrible! Carl didn't know about talent. He just loved that little girl." Executives from Disney came to audition kids for the 1994 film *Blank Check*, about a twelve-year-old who somehow cashes a check for a million dollars. Drew Elliott recalls Carl sitting in on the audition. "Let him do it again!" Carl said. "Let him do it again!" And parents, convinced of their children's talent, sparked to Carl's go-get-'em-kid moxie.

Glenn Close, Joan Lunden, Meat Loaf—they all sent their children to Stagedoor Manor in the '90s. Aerosmith's Steven Tyler did, too—dropping his daughter Mia off in a white stretch limousine. Richard Dreyfuss famously requested permission to drop his kids off in a helicopter. (Denied.) Bryce Dallas Howard, Ron Howard's daughter (who starred in 2009's *Terminator: Salvation*), was a camper in 1996. "I remember there were mothers on the first day of camp who said to their children, 'Become friends with her and her dad will put you in a movie,'" Bryce recalls. "That's been everywhere. But it was more heightened at Stagedoor. Natalie Portman and I were playing opposite each other in *A Midsummer Night's Dream*. And she was a bit protective of me. She told me, 'Hang with this group. This group is very real. They're not going to try to use you.'"

Kim Grigsby, later the music director for Broadway's *Spring Awakening*, was the music director for a handful of shows at Stagedoor Manor in these years, and once worked with a Page Six–worthy cast.

Natalie Portman and Bryce Dallas Howard starred in a 1996 production of *A Mid-summer Night's Dream*. The director, John Stefaniuk (now the associate director of Disney Theatricals's *The Lion King*), remembers Natalie's dedication to her craft. "Her character had fallen asleep in the woods," he says. "In rehearsal one day, Natalie rolled around in the mud to prepare for the scene."

"I had Jacob Bernstein and Jennie Eisenhower in the same show," Kim says. "That's Nixon's granddaughter and Carl Bernstein's son—on the same stage. I was sitting in rehearsals and thinking, *Does anyone else see the irony in this*?" (In a phone call, Nora Ephron doesn't mention the potentially awkward business of running into a Nixon in Loch Sheldrake. Rather, she offered this: "Stagedoor Manor is an amazing place, but it's not easy to get to. I always say to my friends with young children, 'Pick a camp within an hour of New York.'")

Elsie Samuelson, for her part, may have been tickled by the well-known surnames passing through Stagedoor Manor in the '90s, but she didn't suffer any delusions that these celebrities were any better than the rest of us. Her job was still the same: to take care of the children. And in the same way that gay teenagers came to Stagedoor to escape the struggles of their suburban reality, so too did the offspring of celebrities. "I came to Stagedoor for all nine weeks," says Bijou Phillips, daughter of John Phillips (of the Mamas and the Papas). "My dad had a liver transplant when I was nine. He had cancer. He was in and out of the hospital. I was going through a rough time at home." One summer, when John Phillips showed up stinking of alcohol, Elsie gave him a stern talking to. "Elsie was appalled," says her son-in-law, Jonathan Samen. "How he could do this to this poor child. In the off-season, Bijou used to call Carl and Elsie at all hours of the night."

There was a parallel story going on. "Stagedoor Manor was the island of lost toys," says Eric Nightengale, who worked at the camp in the '90s. "Kids who were ignored. Kids who had no community in their high schools. They came to Stagedoor. They were desperate to be challenged, and have someone ask more of them than was being asked of them anywhere else."

For a generation of campers, Carl and Elsie Samuelson were surrogate grandparents. "Carl was like Fred Flintstone," says Gordon Greenberg. And had his own catchphrases. Good things were "huge." Productions weren't great, they were "monumental!"

And like all grandparents, Carl liked to be the hero.

When Jane Ohringer, an early camper, opened on Broadway in 1978, in the original company of *Evita* (playing Perón's mistress), Carl somehow scraped together the money to buy out an entire row of the theater. With the large-scale success of Stagedoor Manor came more generosity. When Jon Cryer opened in *Torch Song Trilogy* in 1985, Carl took fifteen people to Sardi's for dinner to celebrate without thinking twice. "You never saw a check when you were with Carl," says David Quinn, an early camper and close friend of the Samuelsons. "But it was more than that. You didn't feel like the restaurant was even *charging* you."

On show weekends, Carl would throw these parties in the cafeteria in honor of the camp's chef, Jack Ruyack. "You've never seen a spread like this," says Carl's daughter Cindy. Key lime pie. Chocolate cake. "It was like Willy Wonka on steroids." The cook—beloved by everyone—would appear in his white coat to press the flesh with parents. But Jack Ruyack didn't actually bake any of these desserts. They were brought in from local shops. Carl just wanted him to have his moment. "Carl is the one who solved your problems," says Barbara Fine Martin, Stagedoor's highly respected director (a woman who handles every nonartistic detail of the summer so that the creative types are free to do their jobs).

Carl was a larger-than-life figure in the local Liberty, New York, community, too. In the late '90s, Paul Kasofsky (who sold carpet to Stagedoor Manor for years) was building a small shopping center; the plans called for an ice-cream parlor, a Laundromat, and a car wash. But the project was behind schedule, and Paul faced some cash flow issues. Carl owed Paul $2,200 for some carpet that had just been delivered to camp; without prompting, he cut Paul a check for $12,200—an interest-free loan. Paul returned the money immediately with a note that said thanks, but no thanks. "Still, what Carl did was more important to me than the money," Paul says. "It showed we had a wonderful friendship."

Still, like any parent, there was a dark side to Carl. Michael Larsen (who taught at the camp for some twenty-four years) suggests Carl was the type to use his generosity as a cudgel. And he'd pit staff members against each other simply to remind people who was in charge. When Michael was considering leaving Stagedoor in the wake of Jack Romano's death, he approached Carl to talk it out. "Carl would say to me, 'We'll miss you, but we'll get along just fine without you,'" Michael recalls. "But Elsie, she was one of the great women of the century. She was like Beatrice Arthur. After I played a show, Elsie would take my hands and say, 'Oh, what you've given us!' Sometimes you need to hear that. And I never heard it from Carl."

Jonathan Samen, Cindy's husband and a well-respected lawyer in Boston, confirms that view of Carl. This man may have been handing out the checks, but it was Elsie who was pulling the strings behind the scenes. "Without saying too much," Samen says, "Carl's best qualities sprang from Elsie. She was telling Carl what to do. She was the heart and soul of the place. She was the conscience of the camp."

To remember Elsie is to remember a funny story, says Barbara Fine Martin.

Elsie was the bad cop to Carl's good cop. One afternoon, Elsie grabbed the camp's public address system and shouted into the microphone, "So-and-so to the office." Elsie thought she'd taken her thumb off the broadcast button, but she hadn't. And so across Stagedoor's campus one could hear Elsie mutter, "I hate that little bitch." In 1995, another child came to the office begging Elsie to open the canteen so he could get some ice cream. "If you don't open the canteen," the boy said, "I'm going to shoot myself!"

"Get the gun," Elsie said. "I'll help."

Barb describes Elsie as "cotton surrounded by copper wire."

"She was a crab," says Drew Elliott. "But you could turn that scowl into a smile in two seconds." It's worth noting that while Elsie cared for Bijou Phillips with her whole heart, it was not to the detriment of all others. When push came to shove, Elsie kicked Bijou out of camp for a host of offenses, including robbing the canteen. (There are no hard feelings. To this day, Bijou will get drunk with Stagedoor friends and make them run through full sections of the Our Time Cabaret. "It's embarrassing," says Drew, who doesn't drink but still humors her. "She made me do the 'What a Country' dance at this fancy restaurant, Prana, in Las Vegas—for fifty people.")

Elsie had her own desk in the camp's office, where—dressed in her bejeweled track suits—she surrounded herself with postcards from former campers. She'd sit there, filling out her *TV Guide* crossword puzzles, perched next to her famous candy dish. Elsie had a sweet

Elsie Samuelson behind her desk in the camp's main office. "Parents felt comfortable sending their kids to Stagedoor," says Elsie's daughter, Cindy Samuelson. "because they knew my mother would take care of them like her own."

tooth, but the dish was really a ploy to get the kids to visit her. Children would come to grab a piece of candy, Elsie figured. And if they were homesick or in trouble, sooner or later they'd let slip what was really on their mind. Happy or sad, Elsie could see for herself.

David Quinn grew up in Great Neck, Long Island. His father was a diet doctor—one of the first, really—until, that is, the feds came to investigate his practice. David's father dropped him off at Stagedoor Manor one summer, said "See you soon," and disappeared for more than two decades. Elsie, in many ways, adopted David. "This is your home now," she told him. When another camper, Pam Fisher (now an agent at Buchwald & Associates in Los Angeles), lost her mother, Elsie sat next to Pam at the funeral. Elsie turned to Pam, took her hand, and said, "I'll be your mother now." And Elsie followed through on every promise.

"If Carl was larger than life," Konnie says, "Elsie was ten times bigger. Everybody adored her." And famous or infamous (the mobster Joey Gallo's daughter attended Stagedoor), talented or not, Elsie welcomed them all.

One summer in the mid-'90s, Ellen Kleiner gave a campus tour to a conservatively dressed woman and her daughter. "It looked like they'd just come from church," Ellen says. Anyway, Ellen was talking up the facilities, explaining about the food and such at Stagedoor, when a curious boy dressed in fishnet stockings, short black shorts, a studded wrist cuff and a matching collar turned the corner. "He was also wearing perfectly applied women's makeup," Ellen says. "As if he was going to a formal affair. And he was gorgeous!" Ellen wasn't sure what she'd say to this mother if she asked for an explanation. Luckily, the moment passed without incident. Ellen handed this woman and her daughter a Stagedoor brochure and sent them on their way. Meanwhile, back in the office, Ellen, still laughing, relayed the story to Elsie—who grabbed the microphone to the camp's PA system and screamed for that boy to come down to the office. A minute later, the kid in the studded collar appeared in the doorway, asking: "What's wrong?"

Elsie stood there, with her hands on her hips, and looked this boy with the perfectly applied cosmetics up and down. "Take off the fishnets!" Elsie said.

"That's it?" Ellen Kleiner says now, laughing. "The fishnets?"

Elsie was not exactly progressive. This is the woman, after all, who used to go to dress rehearsals for the Our Time Cabaret to make sure the hemlines on the girls's skirts weren't too short. What this story is about, really, is that particular boy and Elsie's need to protect him from the world. "That boy in fishnets came from a very religious family," Barb says. "Elsie knew that to tell him to take off the makeup and the regalia would have destroyed him. For Elsie, removing the fishnets was a compromise." He could be himself at Stagedoor. The sad coda to that story is that when the boy's older sister later asked him if he was gay, and he answered that he thought he was, she lashed out: "If you ever say that again I'll never let you see your niece and nephew."

"That boy never came back to camp after that summer," Barb says.

———

In 1993, Elsie Samuelson was diagnosed with pancreatic cancer—an aggressive, difficult cancer to treat. The doctors gave her just a few months to live. But they underestimated her resolve. Elsie underwent an operation and the cancer went into remission. She thought she was out of the woods, but in 1999 the cancerous cells returned, multiplying at an alarming rate. Elsie underwent several rounds of chemotherapy and was certainly in pain, but she wasn't one to burden others with endless talk of hospitals and treatments. Instead she talked about traveling, and where she and Carl might go next. She talked about her grandchildren (Cindy's kids, now campers at Stagedoor, whom she'd call down to the office every evening for a goodnight kiss). Elsie continued to go antiquing. She loved to buy presents. "She liked to collect things," says Jonathan Samen. "She wanted me to have a collection, even though I didn't *want* a collection. She started buying me little statues of lawyers from around the world. She bought me a little barrister from Italy."

"But she was dying," Konnie says, "and she knew it."

As the disease worsened, support came pouring in from unlikely corners. When Elsie stopped eating—a side effect of the chemotherapy—the owner of Frankie & Johnnie's Restaurant in nearby Hurleyville (it was one of Elsie's favorite establishments) sent over trays of food, night after night, hoping the smell might tempt Elsie to at least take a bite of something. Others responded similarly. For years, Elsie used to go to Zikaren's, a restaurant supply outfit nearby camp to order paper goods and cleaning supplies for the summer. "She would tell me about the shows," says Shirley Zikaren. "She talked about the

camp. She and Carl worked at that business. It didn't just happen."
When Elsie grew too sick to make the ten-minute drive to Zikaren's,
Shirley came to Elsie.

Elsie had bouts of strength. She underwent an experimental form
of treatment for the cancer, developed by Dr. Gregory H. Ripple in
New Hampshire. "There was always the hope that she would dodge
this," says Jonathan. "That she'd be one of the lucky ones."

"She had thumbed her nose at every medical doctor's assessment
of what her future was," says Pam Fisher. "But she was suffering at the
end. She couldn't fight anymore." In their last phone conversation in
the winter of 1999, Konnie said to Elsie: "In case you don't call again,
don't worry. I'll take care of the place. And the candy jar."

On November 26, 1999, Elsie Samuelson—the camp mother, Carl's
devoted wife—passed away at age seventy-two. Her funeral, held three
days later at the Rye Community Synagogue, drew a fifty-five-car pro-
cession. "I don't know how the word even got out," says Debra. "We
told people not to come. That was the line: 'Don't come.'"

A memorial was held at Kutsher's Hotel & Country Club on July
23, 2000. Julia Murney sang "Brother, Can You Spare a Dime." Members of the Our Time Cabaret, from all different eras, performed
together. Barbara Fine Martin, the camp's director, spoke. It was a
particularly moving tribute; in a camp of extroverts and performers,
Barb was the least theatrical, the one behind the scenes, the motor that
kept the place running. But she spoke beautifully of Elsie, whom she
would always remember sitting behind that desk in the office. For
twenty-five years, Barb said, people had come to the camp office, and
their eyes immediately went to Elsie's desk. "She's done more than
most of us have in this life," Barb said. "She carved out a corner of the
world. That corner in the office is Elsie's place."

After an often-teary two hours, Carl (dressed modestly, and clearly moved) made his way to the stage. There was a standing ovation. "I

haven't prepared a speech," Carl said, pausing to collect his thoughts. He told a story instead: One night, he and Elsie had gone to Brown's Hotel to see the Our Time Cabaret perform. Elsie was beaming that night, he recalled, and she was applauding the loudest. An old lady at the next table noticed and leaned over, asking Elsie, "Which of the children is yours?"

"All of them," Elsie replied, without hesitation.

"Elsie tolerated me for forty-nine years, five months, and twenty-six days," Carl said at the memorial. "Neither one of us is perfect. What we got from you guys is perfect."

In the wake of Elsie's death, Carl largely retreated from the camp. He'd sit at his desk, he'd kiss his granddaughters hello, but he wasn't involved in the day-to-day in any substantive way. He didn't need to be. Stagedoor was a well-oiled machine by this point. Enrollment was way up. And Todd Graff's movie *Camp*, based on his experiences at Stagedoor Manor, was released in 2003, only upping the camp's Q-rating further.

That same year, the filmmaker Alexandra Shiva came to Stagedoor Manor to film a documentary. In an hour-long interview, Carl reflected on his life at Stagedoor. "If you do something you love, you're not working," he said. "I haven't worked in forty years." He appeared content, but the interview was tough for him in parts. Carl was ill himself. He'd had a pacemaker implanted earlier that summer, and he was having trouble breathing.

On April 20, 2004—five years after Elsie passed away—Carl suffered a stroke. Internal bleeding led to death. He was seventy-seven years old. Another memorial. Another devastating heartbreak.

Suddenly people were asking: What would happen to Stagedoor Manor?

Just as Jack Romano's death seemed fated—the outspoken, controversial teacher dies just as political correctness is settling in—it is fitting that Carl Samuelson passed away in 2004, just as the country was going down a rabbit hole. *American Idol* was strengthening its deathgrip on pop culture, teaching kids that fame and fortune were not just imminent, but somehow *owed* to them. Entitlement was the prevailing attitude. "We get a lot of kids who want it *now*," says Barb. "They see *American Idol*—where it all happens in twelve weeks and boom! These kids say, 'This is my second year at camp and I want my head shots. And where can my mother get an agent for me?' I see a lot more of that than I used to. In the older days, the kids were happy to have a place to perform." But these reality show narrative arcs are now in their bones.

Dana Steingold, who left Stagedoor in 2002 for the University of Michigan, recently starred in the national tour of the *25th Annual Putnam County Spelling Bee*. In 2009, she returned to camp to talk to the kids about a career in the theater. "They asked the most sophisticated questions," Dana says. "They talked about what 'type' they were. 'I'm a Sutton Foster type.' 'I'm a Kristin Chenoweth type.' I didn't know about *type* when I was a kid at Stagedoor. Or even when I was auditioning for colleges. I just picked my songs and sang. I was my own type." Brent Wagner, the chair of Michigan's musical theater department, has heard this often in very recent years—a shift in self-awareness among applicants—and he expresses dismay at the revelation: "It's smart to know where you fit in. But I wouldn't want someone to feel like that's their destiny at quite a young age. What was a Kristin Chenoweth type before there was a Kristin Chenoweth?"

Carl had seen the way the wind was blowing. The boldface names at Stagedoor in the '90s attracted more talent scouts. "The camp turned into a farm," says the casting director Mark Saks. And the staff had their own ideas about where the camp should go in this new era, about how best to harness the camp's professional momentum and growing cachet. One of the camp's longtime directors suggested Stagedoor Manor actually start auditioning prospective campers before the summer began, weeding out the least talented kids. Carl hated the idea. In a 1999 interview with *InTheater* magazine, he said, "An audition implies, 'What can a camper give us?' What's more important is, 'What can we give them?'"

Carl was proud of the camp's artistic program, certainly. When *Vanity Fair* profiled Natalie Portman in 1999, and the writer suggested Natalie had "never had so much as an acting lesson," Carl was miffed. He gave a quote to the New York *Daily News*, saying: "Natalie did take acting lessons here and was taught theater. She was even in our Master Class." But while he enjoyed playing Broadway Danny Rose, ask Carl about Stagedoor Manor's mission, and he wouldn't talk about talent scouts or managers or agents. He'd quote *Hamlet:* "This above all: to thine own self be true, And it must follow, as the night the day, Thou canst not then be false to any man."

"That's what they're discovering," Carl says, in an outtake from *Stagedoor.* "That's what life should be."

Shortly before his death in 2004, Carl sat down with Barb, saying: "You are going to have to make a decision about which direction you want this camp to go in. Do you want to stay a summer camp or do you want to move in the direction of professional theater?"

"But once Carl died," Barb says, "there was no decision to make. It was a snowball going down the hill. In those first summers, I felt like I was betraying Carl."

The Samuelson daughters—Cindy and Debra—had visited Loch Sheldrake often in the thirty years since their parents woke up one day in 1975 and decided to open a theater camp. Cindy had gotten married, moved to Boston, and had three children of her own, giving up a successful marketing career to focus on her artwork. (She shows at the Blue Heron gallery in Wellfleet, Massachusetts.) Debra was a lawyer working in New York City. They both had fond memories of the camp, and a growing attachment to theater. At Cindy's house, if someone asked "Where are you going?" she was just as likely to answer "Barcelona" (a lyric from *Company*) than anything else. Debra remembers painting scenery that first summer in Loch Sheldrake because she wanted to be a part of it all, and because it was late and someone had to do it. Ask Debra about Stagedoor Manor and she'll talk about watching *Law & Order* reruns in the middle of the night, and laughing "when a former camper shows up." But neither daughter had expressed much interest, at least publicly, in taking over the business.

Yet with their parents suddenly gone, that's exactly what happened. ("I was shocked!" says Cookie Saposnick, who worked in the Stagedoor Manor office for a decade and was one of the camp's first hires.) It was a drastic change in the sisters' commitment, but neither hesitated. "Stagedoor is a family, not a business," Cindy says. And that was that. A plan was hashed out: Cindy would take the lead, handling the day-to-day each summer. Her husband, Jonathan, would be responsible for the legal, accounting, and business side of Stagedoor. And Debra would consult, coming up every weekend each summer.

Eight weeks after her father's death, Cindy, forty-something, moved into Tara, the decidedly quaint house at Stagedoor Manor that her mother had nicknamed after the estate in *Gone With the Wind*. "My daughters were juniors in high school," Cindy says. "And I left town before they'd finished the school year." The transition was jarring for the whole family, and that first summer was particularly crippling. "Every place I looked, I saw my dad," Cindy says.

The improvements the daughters made—at least initially—were largely cosmetic. When it rained (as it does almost daily in the Catskills), Todd Roberts, the head of the costume shop, used to come downstairs in the middle of the night to put out buckets to catch the water. "We did seven roofs in four years," Debra says. The daughters didn't just fix roofs, they shored up the building's foundation, adding additional support in several spots. They replaced every window in the main building. The place needed it. Brad Simmons, a director who worked at the camp for much of the aughts, recalls these years. He lived in a room on the third floor of the main building. "And the floor would give," he says. "It would *give*! Like you might put your foot through it."

The new owners spent hundreds of thousands of dollars rewiring these old buildings and installing an up-to-date fire alarm system. The importance of these upgrades cannot be overstated. "Carl didn't fix anything," says Ellen Kleiner. "It was always Band-Aids. This is a true story: Studio B was leaking. It always leaked. One summer, it was absolutely pouring in. The maintenance man took out the ceiling tiles to see what was going on—and he found a bathtub. In the ceiling! There was a hole in the roof, and someone had installed a bathtub in the ceiling to catch the water. A pipe was attached to the bathtub, and it drained out somewhere. I remember standing there thinking, I mean, *A bathtub in the ceiling*. You didn't even know what to say." (Ellis Marmor, Stagedoor's steward and a summer camp veteran who'd been close to Carl, clarifies the thought process behind his old friend's patchwork approach to maintenance. "Carl hadn't always been comfortable in his life," Ellis says. "Now that he had some money, he wanted to keep it that way.")

Stagedoor Manor celebrated its thirtieth anniversary in 2005 with a star-studded showcase at nearby Kutsher's Hotel. It was hard to believe neither Carl nor Elsie was there. "Their legacy will be the opportunity they gave to all of these kids," says Drew Elliott. The Samuelsons would have been proud of the turnout. Zach Braff and Mandy Moore, both Stagedoor alums, dating at the time, showed up arm in arm. "I went to the thirtieth anniversary with my wife," Michael Ian Black says. "Michael Larsen was in the main theater playing the piano. There were probably fifty or sixty former campers of varying ages standing around the piano singing through the whole Our Time Cabaret. It was the corniest thing I have ever seen. It was also one of the most joyful and uplifting. And that's what Stagedoor is: a combination of joyful, uplifting, and corny. Mostly corny."

In the winter of 2007, in their first large-scale initiative since taking over the camp, Cindy and Debra converted Stagedoor's indoor pool into a high-end theater—a massive, million-dollar undertaking. No one used the indoor pool, they figured, and it was increasingly expensive to maintain. "I'm on board now with the changes," says Barb. "But Carl never would have paved over the indoor pool. He never wanted Stagedoor to be anything but a summer camp. How many camps have an indoor pool? It didn't matter that we used it once a session. It was a selling point."

"My father was not intransigent," Cindy says. "He looked at things and said, 'Does this make sense?' Yes, the indoor pool was a selling point. But the camp was full. We had a waiting list. It was obvious the pool wasn't being used. It was deteriorating and it cost a lot of money to maintain. He would have been fine with closing the pool."

———

In a way, this push-and-pull is the story of this century's first decade, when everything went corporate. The camp was still a mom-and-pop operation, run by the daughters of the original owner, but it was a family business for the new millennium. If Stagedoor changed in the coming years, it was merely responding to the culture at large—to yet another shift in expectations among both parents and children.

In the '90s, every parent believed his or her child was a star. That may still be true. But these parents are now much better educated—and more realistic—having spent the last decade watching *American Idol*. They're now keenly aware that while their own child may be talented, there are a million other talented kids just like them out there (all willing to sleep outside for a shot at being insulted on national television). And so Stagedoor—once the place you sent your kid

The indoor pool at Stagedoor Manor was a nice selling point, and was prominently featured in Carl's brochures. But with the exception of a 1992 camp production of Stephen Sondheim's musical *The Frogs*—which was staged in the pool—the thing was rarely used.

Over the winter of 2007, the indoor pool was converted into a high-tech theater in the round. Cindy Samuelson (seen here in the renovated space), christened the new venue, the Oasis Theater.

to find a manager—was now just one step on the long road to helping a child achieve that dream.

The change among campers was more dramatic. Carl used to quote Hamlet: "To thine own self be true." But the camp needed a new lesson. Because these kids—living in an America where you could come out in high school, likely without incident, where you could submit your auditions to casting directors on YouTube—knew who they were. And more important what they wanted: an intensive summer training program.

To that end, under the new regime, Stagedoor's artistic program was amped up. Players Ensemble, the dramatic equivalent of the Our Time Cabaret, was introduced. The audition-only dramatic troupe would meet every afternoon for two hours, crafting a show of short scenes culled from a range of plays. In 2008, Stagedoor also introduced Dramafest, a playwriting competition for campers—produced in conjunction with Stephen Sondheim's Young Playwrights, Inc. (This harked back to a Jack Romano program, Festival Week, where playwrights like Jonathan Marc Sherman and Ivan Menchell got their start.) Suddenly, for these kids, being in a drama—as opposed to the more high-profile Stagedoor musicals—didn't mean you were a second-class citizen. In these years, the minimum age for campers was upped from eight to ten, because the program was becoming too intense for the youngest kids. (Jon Foster, star of ABC's *Accidentally On Purpose*, was one of the last eight-year-olds at camp. His older brother, *3:10 to Yuma*'s Ben Foster, watched over him. "My roommate was crying hysterically," Jon recalls. "He said, 'I'm sick of camp and I'm sick of you!' He put a black jelly bean on my pillow and said it was rat poop. I was in *Joseph and the Amazing Technicolor Dreamcoat*. Just before the show, someone told me, 'These people called managers and agents will be watching the play. Do a good job.' I thought, *I don't know what you're talking about and I'll just go out there and do what the director has been telling me to do for the last couple of weeks*.")

Lest one think the revolution was merely theoretical, the revised credo was suddenly in writing. One of Carl's favorite phrases to describe Stagedoor was, *The only summer camp of its kind*. It had adorned the literature. Still did. But now every reference to "summer camp" was taken out of the camp's promotional materials. Instead Stagedoor was referred to exclusively by its original (and formal) name, the Stagedoor Manor Performing Arts Training Center. And it was, legitimately, that. "The place has credibility," says Bernie Telsey, a top Broadway casting director, whose credits include *Rent, The Drowsy Chaperone*, and many others. "Kids who come out of there—you know they can sing. And it doesn't feel like one of those teens-put-on-a-show fake acting."

It was tough to argue with the numbers. The summer after Carl died was the first time Stagedoor had a waiting list. The camp now sells out nine months in advance. In 2009, there were two hundred names on the waiting list—enough to open a second camp, it should be noted. (A bit of trickle-down economics: there's also now a waiting list at the Lazy Pond Bed & Breakfast in nearby Liberty, considered *the* place to stay on performance weekends. This is where the mother of Jonah Hill—he of *Superbad* fame—stays when she drops off her daughter.) "I get offered bribes all the time," Barb says. "I've had parents say, 'I've got two checks, one for $4,945. How much should I write the other one for?' Demi Moore's kid was on the waiting list!"

Shortly after her father died, Cindy stopped advertising altogether. "We didn't need it," she said. Instead she hired a publicist, a former camper named Amy Brownstein, "I felt very strongly that we were a well-kept secret," Cindy says. A spot on NBC's *Today* show soon followed, as did a story in *People* magazine. ("Carl's idea of publicity was sending a few photographs to a camper's local town newspaper," Barb says.) As sure a sign as any of Stagedoor's unprecedented popularity, in 2008, four new rooms were built onto the *boys'* dorm. It was a far cry from the 1980s, when Stagedoor Manor had to offer substantial scholarships just to get boys through the front door.

The camp was suddenly on the radar of professional organizations in Manhattan in ways that would have been inconceivable to Carl. The thing is that Stagedoor is not just a place to be discovered. It's now a place for multinational corporations to workshop new material. In 2006, Disney Theatricals began the long process of repurposing the mega-hit movie *High School Musical* for the stage, hoping to launch a national tour. If successful, high schools and community theaters would line up to license the show. But would *HSM* even work on stage? Would the show need more songs? A fleshed-out script? To find out, Disney turned to Stagedoor Manor for a trial run. The campers had less than three weeks to put up the show. It was not a simple transition. Bryan Louiselle, the original *HSM* writer, penned two new songs, "Cellular Fusion" and "Counting on You," for the Stagedoor production. Steve Fickinger, the vice president of licensing for Disney Theatricals, drove up to Stagedoor for the premiere—with twelve members of his team in tow. They made notes. They whispered. If what they saw wasn't a finished product, it was enough to glimpse what it *could* be. "Never underestimate the value in just getting the thing up," says Fickinger. In the two years that followed, *High School Musical* would be performed at more than two thousand schools across the country, not to mention the Equity national and international tours.

"We were the ship that launched it all," says Stagedoor's Larry Nye.

These opportunities are now part of the DNA of Stagedoor Manor. In 2007, campers at Stagedoor Manor participated in a youth-friendly adaptation of *Sweeney Todd,* with Sondheim himself e-mailing changes to the score. Which is to say, what these children do is no longer happening in a vacuum.

Careerism aside, in some ways, these kids haven't changed at all. They may talk about their prescription medications over lunch, but like Jack Romano's most die-hard students, their hearts still beat to the rhythms of Rodgers & Hammerstein. It's the *culture* that's changed, and maybe jaded these kids. In 2009, on the second day at Stagedoor, a panel discussion was held for the entire camp in the Elsie Theater, consisting of an agent from Buchwald & Associates, the casting director for the Broadway musical *13*, and the New York talent agent Nancy Carson. The panel was moderated by a Stagedoor director and it was an informative afternoon—though it's unclear what the ten-year-olds sitting in the front row must have thought when the moderator opened the session with this highly specific question: "We all want to know, What's the difference between an agent and a manager?"

When a casting director for FX's *Damages* and another for Kansas City Rep (scouting for an upcoming production of *Into the Woods* directed by Moisés Kaufman) passed through Stagedoor one week later, two girls from the Our Time Cabaret practically ignored them. "Casting directors come all the time," one said. "It's not a big deal." There's a reason shows like *The Me Nobody Knows* and *Runaways*—so popular in Jack's era—no longer held sway over these kids. Their real lives are bigger than those fictional characters.

The Internet erased the physical distance between theater geeks. And this generation—reared on MTV's *Real World*, which arguably did more for sexual freedom than *Will & Grace*—was more secure in their identities. Todd Buonopane attended Stagedoor in the early '90s. "I came out of the closet at fourteen," he says. "I told my mom it wasn't a big deal, because it wasn't. There were gay couples at camp who were like other married couples." Todd was something of a pioneer in his day. Now, the coming-out story isn't even part of these kids' stripes. In some cases, that declaration happens between commercial breaks. This generation of theater geeks is post-gay. At a Stagedoor rehearsal, if a director is taking attendance, instead of announcing "here" a gay kid might say "queer." They're out in high school, out to their parents. Yet they'd rather not be out in print, for fear of what it might do to their career. Perhaps that's not all that surprising. When the musical *Chicago* opened on Broadway in 1975, it was seen as sharp critique of political corruption in the judicial system. In 2002, when the movie opened—with Richard Gere and Renée Zellwegger—it was interpreted as a treatise on tabloid culture. Same musical. Different generational lens.

These kids are in some ways infinitely more mature than their predecessors, but they are lost in other ways. When cell phone use became rampant at camp, the Stagedoor brass started taking the phones away for the first week. It wasn't so much that they were afraid the kids would call their parents and complain. Rather, they wanted them to unplug and reconnect to their environment. The policy became dogma when, one summer not long ago, in the midst of a crippling asthma attack, a female camper called her mother a hundred miles away to ask what she should do. "Uh, open your door and get a counselor!" her mother replied.

While the professional opportunities increased exponentially, Cindy and this new regime managed to push back—hoping to create some balance. Under Jack Romano and Michael Larsen, there'd been a clear distinction between the Our Time Cabaret kids and the less talented campers. The OTC kids would convene in the lobby—dressed in their red, black, and white—before heading out to entertain at Kutsher's and Brown's. The other kids looked on, the jealousy seeping through their overactive teenage pores. The cabaret gave the other kids something to strive toward. But hearts were broken. Taryn Glist attended Stagedoor from 1989 to 1996, and was selected for the cabaret early on. Later, at Emerson College, she met a girl from the same Stagedoor era. "I didn't remember her," Taryn says. "She made a comment, 'You wouldn't know me. I wasn't in the cabaret.' It was one of the first times it became apparent to me: It was almost two camps. There was the crew I was a part of, and the crew I didn't know."

The new administration has gone to great lengths to close this gap, introducing other programs to celebrate kids, both as dramatic actors and as writers. Previously, the Our Time Cabaret was for the best campers—of any age, from ten to eighteen. Now it's mostly for the oldest kids, mostly something you expect to join in your final years. It's a telling change.

"I believe that seeing someone collapse on the floor in tears, to really want something desperately and not get it—that in and of itself is an enormous lesson to have as a thirteen-year-old," says Eric Nightengale, founder of Manhattan's 78th Street Lab Theater, who directed at Stagedoor Manor in the '90s. He has a unique perspective on the evolution of the camp, having returned in 2008 for one summer after a decade away. "Jack Romano was product oriented," Eric says. "He would stack the casts, and the kids were aware of the politics of that. If you were in Jack's cabaret, you could flagrantly break the rules. That was the gestalt of the camp." But under Cindy's direction, the counselors have a curfew. The staff is discouraged from yelling—that's written into the rule book.

"With Cindy in charge," Nightengale says, "your first thought when making a decision is always, *How is this going to impact the kids?* Some of the camp's explosive energy is gone. But it's a much healthier environment."

CHAPTER 7

Hell Week

IN THE FINAL WEEK AT STAGEDOOR MANOR, CLASSES ARE phased out entirely. The casts rehearse for eight hours every day. "It's like Equity rehearsals," one director says. "Eight-hour days with breaks for food." Hence the nickname: Hell Week.

It's common for directors to "act-swap" with other shows throughout Hell Week. For example, during an afternoon rehearsal, the cast of *Sweeney Todd* might perform their act one for the cast of *Into the Woods,* and vice versa. No props, no sets, just a down-and-dirty gypsy run-through for a supportive audience of good friends—just as professional companies do. In William Goldman's *The Season,* the late George Abbott explains the importance of such displays. As a director, you have some sense of what works—if a dance is particularly moving, or a piece of acting exciting. "But you don't really know much without an audience," Abbott says. "You have to get hot bodies out there to be able to tell."

The excitement of Hell Week 2009 is hampered, however, by a virus running amok through camp, sending kids to the infirmary at an alarming rate. One feels awful for these run-down thespians. (Is there anything worse than a sick kid at summer camp?) Yet there is a tinge of humor in seeing the Wolf from *Into the Woods* in bed next to Riff from *West Side Story,* down the hall from the Acid Queen from *The Who's Tommy.* In an effort to nip this sudden epidemic in the bud, children are no longer allowed to serve themselves in the cafeteria; the metal serving spoons like Petri dishes. Use of Purell hand sanitizers, installed in the cafeteria a few years back, is now mandatory for staff and campers alike upon entrance and exit. And the communal supply of breakfast cereals (like a horse's trough filled with Lucky Charms) has been replaced with comparably sanitary, single-serving disposable bowls.

Dress rehearsals are fast approaching—for *Into the Woods,* for *Sweeney Todd,* for *A Funny Thing Happened on the Way to the Forum,* for all fourteen shows—whether these casts are ready or not. The unspoken (but obvious) question on everyone's mind is: Will the shows get up?

The performance weekend is coming on so quickly, there is nary a moment to take a breath, which can only mean one thing: it's time for a montage.

I.

OVERHEARD AT A REHEARSAL FOR SHAKESPEARE'S *A MIDSUMMER NIGHT'S DREAM:* The director, Lawrence Lesher (thirty-something, patient), is dressed in a Washington Nationals T-shirt. "You cannot really do the work," he tells his cast, "until you're off book. Before we break for the night, are there any other questions?"

OBERON: "Yeah, what are the Nationals?"

LAWRENCE: "A Major League Baseball team."

OBERON: "Oh."

2.

Evening recreation: Aaron Albert, a camper departing immi-
nently to film a TV series, fights with his girlfriend. They are the
Brangelina of Stagedoor Manor, and their teenage ups and downs
are chronicled with that same exhausting level of intrigue. Outside the cafeteria, in the heat of a disagreement, Aaron, seventeen, shouts, "I give you the world!"

3.

Players Ensemble rehearsal, Elsie Theater. The camp's audition-
only dramatic troupe. Director Rob Scharlow is out sick. The
stage manager, Elaine, addresses the cast.

ELAINE: "I'll be running rehearsal. Rob's not gonna make it."

CAMPER: [gasp] "He's gonna die?"

ELAINE: "No . . . He's not gonna make it to rehearsal *today.*"

4.

Overheard at Stagedoor Manor, afternoon recreation.

BOY #1: "Where are you from?"

BOY #2: "Manhattan."

BOY #3: "I thought you were from Long Island?"

BOY #2: "I *sleep* on Long Island. But the city is my *home.*"

5.

Players Ensemble rehearsal, Elsie Theater: Two teenage white
girls rehearse a scene from John Patrick Shanley's *Doubt.* It's the
moment in the Pulitzer Prize–winning play when an aging nun
informs a black, single mother that her son may have been sexually abused by a priest. The girl shouts back, "You can't hold a

child responsible for what God gave him to be." Later that evening, the Players Ensemble cast runs through a scene from a new play about genocide in Darfur. It's a moving piece of theater which includes a dramatic description of rape at the hands of the Janjaweed, the armed gunmen pillaging Darfur. Rape? Genocide? One kid issues his gleeful verdict: "This scene is *so* Players!"

6.

There is an *Upstairs, Downstairs* quality to life at summer camp. And while it is the nature of young children to believe their teachers cease to exist after class—that these dedicated men and women simply disappear into thin air once the tap shoes are stowed away—this is of course not true.

At Stagedoor Manor, they disappear to the "library."

The *library* is not a library at all. Unless your local memorial book-stop serves $7 pitchers of domestic beer and chicken fingers. The library's formal name is Bum & Kel's Lakeside Tavern, a bar and grill on the shores of Loch Sheldrake. What's the crowd like? "Some have teeth," says Larry Nye, the head of Stagedoor's dance department. "It's male-heavy. Blue-collar. A lot of them are prison guards. There's a prison thirty minutes away. We're the summer folk. They tolerate us."

Though the camp's staff goes to great lengths to conceal their nighttime activities from the kids, some of the more in-the-know campers like Harry Katzman enjoy teasing them. "How was the *library*?" Harry will ask at breakfast. "Check out a lot of *books*?"

7.

Overheard at Stagedoor Manor: "I would take a role in *SVU* for the paycheck."

8.

The lobby. One of Stagedoor's handsome young directors walks by two male campers and waves hello. Once the director is out of earshot, the following conversation unfurls:

BOY #1: "That director? He's my boyfriend."

BOY #2: "No, he's not."

BOY #1: "I know. But [mock hair flip] a girl can dream."

9.

Wednesday, Stagedoor's sandpit, cast-on-cast beach volleyball tournament. The rules? There are no rules. There is no limit to the number of players allowed on the sand at one time, no limit to the number of taps allowed to get the ball back over the net. It's a theatrical free-for-all. The only rule, a twelve-year-old child explains, is to avoid the wire. "If the ball hits that"—he points to the camp's intercom wire—"yell 'Wire!' and there's a do-over." Today, some twenty-seven cast members of *The Drowsy Chaperone*—with tar blackouts drawn beneath their eyes in an ironic nod to the faux-competitive nature of Stagedoor's lone sporting event—take on the cast of *West Side Story*. Barb, the camp's director: "Every summer, I call the athletic supply company and order one volleyball and a couple of cans of tennis balls," she says. "The guy on the phone laughs, '*This* is a summer camp?'"

10.

Lunch, dining room: A staff member addresses the entire camp—staff and children alike—with a concern about the laundry. Apparently, someone accidentally left a red sock in a bag of whites, and the full contents of that bag came back a lovely shade of pink. "Please be careful when you are doing laundry," she says over the lunchroom PA system. "Some people will be upset with pink clothing. [beat] But not everyone!"

11.

Overheard at Stagedoor Manor.

BOY #1: "I saw *August: Osage County* with Phylicia Rashad."

BOY #2: "Who is that?"

BOY #1: "She was in *The Cosby Show*. She was fierce."

BOY #2: [rolling his eyes] "I don't believe in color-blind casting. [beat] Unless it's Audra McDonald."

12.

Sweeney Todd rehearsal, Studio D. In the corner of the room sits a pile of gold, New Year's Eve style party hats. They are props for some show that session, no doubt. But the cast of *Sweeney Todd*, on a break, suddenly takes notice of them. Jordan Firstman picks up a hat, presses it to his chest, and sings, to himself at first: *"One* [pop] . . . *singular sensation, every little step she takes."* He moves through the choreography, so famous from the film of *A Chorus Line*, running his fingertips along the brim of the hat. The musical director, noticing Jordan, picks up the cue and plays along on the piano. One by one, members of the cast join in, until the entire room has wandered over, as if answering a siren call. It is the least self-conscious moment of the entire summer, and a breath of beautiful calm.

13.

Dramafest, Oasis Theater: The entire camp has turned out to watch a performance of five original short plays written by their

Stagedoor peers. The topics of today's works (in no particular order): Alzheimer's, suicide, writer's block, a botched wedding engagement, and Mark David Chapman.

Spotlight on Arielle Baumgarten and Leah Fishbaugh—"the Meryl Streep and Glenn Close of Stagedoor Manor," Konnie says—playing mother and daughter. This play, *The Things We Never Said,* written by seventeen-year-old Austin Sprague, is set in a nursing home. The mother, confronting the depths of dementia, has taken to labeling everything in her hospital room with Post-its.

A welcome bit of (albeit unintentional) levity arrives during the final piece, the one about suicide. The audience, though engaged, can't help but notice that the talented young actor currently breaking down onstage is wearing a navy shirt embossed with a number: 69.

14.

Garden Room, lunch. A rule of thumb: If a boy you've never seen before is suddenly invited to eat a meal in this exclusive section of the cafeteria, there is a good chance it's because a member of the Our Time Cabaret has a crush on him.

15.

Sweeney Todd rehearsal, Studio D: The knives come out. A prop master from the original Broadway production of *Sweeney Todd* drops in to deliver a set of "blades" modeled on the ones Len Cariou used in the show's 1979 premiere. Plastic tarps are laid down. And the cast of *Sweeney Todd* practice slitting each other's throats. Director Jeff Murphy is pleased. "These blades have some weight to them," he says, holding one in his hand. "And the lights will catch on the metal. We've never had blades that looked this menacing." Which is to say the killing won't look like some cartoonish Halloween massacre. Still, Jeff pulls the prop mistress aside: "Should we add a little Karo syrup to make the blood thicker?"

16.

Lobby. Late night. Stagedoor Manor's directors (a community, if there ever was one) console each other. Stephen Agosto—who played LeFou in the national tour of *Beauty and the Beast*—is directing *West Side Story* this session, and he's bleary-eyed. While he has been working tirelessly with his cast in rehearsals, drawing out performances of shocking nuance, he sums up his thoughts on directing a teenage production of *West Side Story:* "I want the parents in and out in ninety minutes. Give them the balcony scene, give them Rita Moreno, give them 'I Feel Pretty,' and if they're still awake in the second act, give them *'Chino, give me the Gun!'* and call it a day."

17.

Monday evening, Jack Romano Playhouse, and a performance of the Our Time Cabaret, the camp's celebrated revue: Jordan Firstman (a talented actor who otherwise plays Sweeney Todd this session) steps forward to sing a snippet of "Being Alive," an emotional plea for companionship from the 1970 musical *Company.* The lyrics, as Sondheim originally wrote them: *"Somebody to hold me too close, Somebody to hurt me too deep, Somebody to sit in my chair, And ruin my sleep, And make me aware of being alive."* Tonight—be it nerves, exhaustion, or a temporary lapse in concentration—Jordan blanks on the words, repeating *"somebody to sit in my chair"* two or three times over the melody. Backstage after the show, there is much hugging and celebrating and applause—before the conversation inevitably turns to teasing Jordan about that infraction. For the rest of the night (and much of the week), his best friends walk around camp, changing the lyrics of every song to *"sit in my chair, to sit in my chair, to sit in my chair."*

18.

Playhouse Theater, a run-through of *West Side Story:* Before the rehearsal, director Stephen Agosto issues one command to his actors: "Every time you come out onstage," he says, "think about *why* you're coming out onstage."

Thirty minutes later, a blackout marks the end of a scene in the bridal shop where Anita works. While there are hired stage-hands at Stagedoor, sometimes the children are asked to take small props on and off. Like now, when a young boy in glasses—one of the Sharks—is asked to quickly remove the dress form from the set.

KID: [pauses]

STEPHEN: "What is it, Boo-Boo?"

KID: "Um, I have a question, Stephen. Why am I coming onstage right now?"

STEPHEN: "To remove the dress form from the shop."

KID: "I know that . . . [innocently] But *why* am I coming on-stage?"

STEPHEN: [beat] "Please take the dress form off of the stage."

19.

Sneak Peek, Elsie Theater, Wednesday evening, two days until Performance Weekend. Sneak Peek is just what it says it is: a first look at that session's fourteen shows. Each cast is invited up on-stage to perform one number in front of the entire camp. John Stefaniuk (who came to Stagedoor in the '90s directly from a post at London's Royal Academy of Dramatic Art, and has since gone on to be the associate director for *The Lion King*) came up with the idea back in 1996, and it's a wonder no one thought of it earlier. These Stagedoor Manor campers spend three weeks rehearsing elaborate shows but almost never get to see their roommates perform.

For Sneak Peek, the directors are instructed to select a group number—so that every kid in the cast will feel included. Yet the program can become a pissing contest between directors. It has been ever thus. "Word would get around very quickly at Stagedoor," Stefaniuk says. "There'd be sleeper hits, and shows to miss." Stefaniuk recalls one camp director—so proud of his own work—leaning over to another and whispering, "Did you see that choreography!" The other, unimpressed, sniffed and replied, "Yeah, I did. Like, forty years ago."

The competitive nature of the evening (among staff, anyway) leads to sometimes surprising scene selections. A few years back, Harry Katzman played Parchester, a supporting role, in *Me and My Girl*. He had only one song in the entire show, "The Family Solicitor." That song didn't introduce the musical, didn't really make sense as a stand-alone piece. But still, that was the number the director chose to put up for Sneak Peek. Why? He knew it was the best thing he had. It's a common occurrence. When Stagedoor mounted Elton John's *Aida* one summer, in rehearsal the music director worked closely with the actress playing the character Amneris. She had a huge voice, but he counseled her to inject some nuance into her performance—to hold something back in a song so she could build to the climax. "Don't give it all away," he'd say in rehearsal. That was smart direction for the show, but not necessarily for Sneak Peek, where the cast has just a few moments to impress. And so, just before the cast of *Aida* went onstage to perform, this music director pulled that very same teenage girl aside to lay down a new law: "Forget what I said in rehearsal. *You better belt your face off tonight.*"

This is just further proof that Stagedoor Manor is a microcosm of the New York theater scene. Consider this: Every summer in Manhattan, casts from the various Broadway shows perform in Bryant Park through a free lunchtime program called Broadway in the Park. "Broadway in the Park is Sneak Peek all over again," Stefaniuk says. "It's like, You go show those *Wicked* people what *real* acting is."

Sneak Peek 2009. Rachael Singer sits upstairs at the Elsie Theater, alongside the cast of *Sweeney Todd*. It is Wednesday evening and just thirty-six hours before her first performance as Mrs. Lovett. Tonight, the *Sweeney* cast is scheduled to perform "The Ballad of Sweeney Todd"—the only number from the show where Rachael's *not* featured. She will stand onstage tonight and sing along, but to be honest, she's happy for the too-harsh glare of the spotlight to shift to someone else for a moment. Because Rachael would be the first to admit that, despite the extra rehearsal time she'd put in these two weeks, she wasn't finding the character. She still didn't understand Mrs. Lovett. The Stagedoor directors may have been preoccupied with tonight's showcase, but Harry, Brian and Rachael were too concerned with their own progress to worry much about bragging rights. If Sneak Peek was a wash this year, so be it.

Rachael wasn't the only one struggling at *Sweeney Todd*. After a particularly unproductive rehearsal, the music director, Justin Mendoza, sat the kids down and explained how disappointed he was with their work ethic and concentration. The cast was ashamed. And Rachael and Jordan—the oldest members, the leaders of the ensemble— felt they were at fault. It was their responsibility to inspire the younger kids. And so they called their own meeting in one of the rehearsal studios to address the cast. The pep rally begins:

"We have a solid show," Jordan said.

"We have to show Jeff and Justin that we care," Rachael added. "That we're willing to take it to the next level."

The actor playing Signor Pirelli spoke up: "As a group, our energy level is amazing. We support each other. We laugh together." There is a lot of head-nodding.

"We need to punch them in the face with our sound," Jordan said. "This could be one of the best shows ever."

Rachael smiled, standing before the cast, playing the veteran. But the truth is, it's unclear that she actually believed what she was saying. She was so lost herself.

At one rehearsal during Hell Week, the director instructed the cast to sit around in a circle and discuss their respective roles. He asked the campers to invent a back-story for their characters. Whether they had starring roles or played nameless ensemble members, every character should have a history, he instructed. A girl in the chorus ran with it, inventing an entire biography for her previously anonymous character. "I was abused at age six," she explained, "and now I'm homeless. And I like to pick up the scraps from Mrs. Lovett's pie shop." It was a wildly detailed profile. Rachael, by contrast, described Mrs. Lovett as "pretty normal" and "bubbly" until "you see her crazy side." The room went quiet. (Shortly thereafter, the director procured a DVD of Angela Lansbury in the original production of *Sweeney Todd*—a sort of digital crib sheet for the young actress.)

Hoping to flesh out the character, Rachael comandeered the Ping-Pong room for a sit-down with her co-star. While their friends sat by the pool tanning themselves or ate ice cream from the canteen, these two actors discussed the relationship between Lovett and Sweeney Todd. *Why does Sweeney Todd refer to London as a "hole in the world"?*

Why is Mrs. Lovett the only person to recognize him? It's character work. They talk about gestures Rachael might incorporate into the pie shop scenes. "What would you do with your hands," Jordan asks her, "if you were baking? Wipe sweat off of your forehead?"

Rachael is hunched over in her chair. The memory of Natalie Walker's triumphant performance as Mrs. Lovett just two years earlier—along with the expectation that Rachael would perform just like Natalie—weighs on her. She has most of the lyrics memorized, but the meaning sometimes eludes her. Take "Poor Thing," in which Mrs. Lovett tells of the tragedies that befell Sweeney Todd's family during his fifteen-year absence. "This song is story telling," the music director explains to Rachael in rehearsal. "If you don't know what you're singing about, you may as well be singing *blah blah blah* on key." The director stops her again. "It's not 'poor thing,'" he says. "It's *pooooor theeeeng. Tooo baahhd.* Mrs. Lovett is a big character." Only adding to the challenge, this song is written in waltz time: *1-2-3, 1-2-3.* For a generation reared on four-four pop music, it's easy to trip over these beats.

During lunch that final week, Rachael is dressed in a zip-up sweatshirt, and she barely takes a bite, just moving a piece of pizza around her plate while refusing to look up from the table. She shrugs her shoulders and wipes away a fistful of tears. "I don't want to let anyone down," she says.

There are teenage girls at Stagedoor Manor who will cry at a costume fitting. Or when the kitchen staff runs out of ham on cold cuts day. But Rachael isn't a drama queen, which makes this sudden display of raw emotion all the more unnerving. "I'm not ready for the dress rehearsal," she says. Unfortunately, she's out of time.

There's a truly magic moment every session at Stagedoor Manor, when a kid goes to sleep at night and comes in to rehearsal twelve hours later to find a hulking set onstage. And suddenly he can see the whole show coming together before his eyes, glimpsing how that grueling work might now pay off. The tech staff often work until three in the morning in these Stagedoor theaters, installing the set pieces before falling into bed. Perhaps they should set an alarm for the next morning; exhaustion be damned, it'd be worth it to see these kids's faces.

During Hell Week, the *Sweeney Todd* set arrives in fits. But there is a Christmas-like atmosphere on the morning of Thursday's dress rehearsal when the elements are finally all in place. Two big metal gates (on wheels) represent the streets of London. And there are columns. Columns that actually look like marble! But the the *pièce de résistance* is a massive cube, some six feet, four inches tall, ten feet long by twelve feet deep. It's a feat of engineering modeled on the original Broadway set. One side of the cube serves as Mrs. Lovett's pie shop, another is decorated as the backdrop to her living room. But climb the stairs to the top of the cube and you'll find yourself in Sweeney Todd's barbershop, complete with a working trapdoor. After the demon barber slits your throat, his chair reclines and the dead body slinks off, disappearing through the floor and down into the oven.

The set would have been awesome for today's dress rehearsal. That is, if the thing actually functioned properly.

The cast of *The Drowsy Chaperone* was invited to sit in on *Sweeney Todd*'s dress rehearsal. The director, Jeff Murphy, apologizes in advance for any technical difficulties they might witness. "We've never run through the show all the way," he explains.

Well, the problems (numerous) begin almost immediately. The opening number is meant to be menacing. The ensemble sings, *"Swing your razor wide, Sweeney! Hold it to the skies! Freely flows the blood of those who moralize!"* Sweeney Todd—center stage, creepy, lit in shadows—is seen disposing of body bags, dumping the corpses through a sewer grate in the stage floor. Unfortunately, the body bags aren't weighted correctly and it looks like he isn't so much disposing of victims as he is making a UPS drop-off. He looks like some deranged Santa Claus, with a shock of gray hair and bloodshot eyes.

The cube, meanwhile, is heavier than anticipated, and it turns slowly—the scene changes between the streets of London and Lovett's pie shop are disastrous. Dragging the thing offstage isn't nearly as simple as imagined, and the first set change takes close to ten minutes. At one point, the director stops the show entirely, instructing the cast—still onstage in front of their friends—to "relax." Of course there's no better audience than one of your peers. And the *Drowsy* cast cheered like mad, despite the interminable set changes and missed cues. Still, there was some crowd fatigue, and who could blame them? The *Sweeney Todd* dress rehearsal ran more than five hours.

Though it's of little comfort to Rachael and the cast, it should be noted that the exact same thing happened at the first preview of *Sweeney Todd* on Broadway in 1979. "We were having a terrible time with the set," star Len Cariou relates in Meryle Secrest's biography of Sondheim. "The barbershop was directly above the pie shop, and the whole thing was supposed to be made of aluminum, so that it could be pushed around, but they had made it out of steel. It weighed a ton and nobody could move it. Every run-through we had to stop. We hadn't gotten to the end for a week, and I said to Hal [Prince] and Steve [Sondheim], 'I have forgotten how this fucking thing ends.'"

Even if Rachael had known that story, it wouldn't have been much comfort. There were other problems today. Rachael flubbed a few lines in "Poor Thing," and the act-one finale, "A Little Priest," whose comedy had such a light touch in rehearsal, failed to land today. The second act opens in Mrs. Lovett's suddenly popular pie shop. (It's made of people! People!) Mrs. Lovett is supposed to be refilling drinks while trying to keep the homeless beggar woman out of the store. But Rachael isn't connected to the scene, isn't reacting to what's in front of her; she's just going through the motions. For example, before she even sees the beggar woman enter, Rachael is already shouting to her assistant, "Toby! *Throw the old woman out!*" The ensemble did not fare much better. During "City on Fire," the music director actually had to stop playing entirely, because the cast was so off tempo.

The ensemble was disappointed—you could see it in their faces, now hanging so much lower than they'd been just a few hours ago when they first glimpsed the set onstage at the Elsie Theater. The director was himself frustrated. Perhaps even more so when one of the ensemble members pulled him aside with what, to the kid anyway, must have seemed like a burning question at the time. "Do we look crazy enough in the asylum scene?" the boy asked.

Rachael and the rest of the cast stumbled into dinner, hopelessly defeated. The dress rehearsal ran so late they had to eat supper in full makeup. Stagedoor is a competitive environment, and Rachael couldn't help but feel that people were staring at her. That the word was out. And the word was not good. A fellow cast member—frazzled, with fake blood still on his clothes—was likewise disturbed, and he approached Rachael to commiserate: "I just heard five people say our show isn't good."

"I don't want to hear it!" Rachael snapped back.

A Funny Thing Happened on the Way to the Forum had a tortured road to Broadway back in 1962. At the show's Washington, D.C., tryout, the company sometimes performed for audiences of less than a hundred people. For a brief moment, the show featured a song called "There's Something About a War." While that song was dropped before the show arrived in New York, well, damn if the sentiment didn't ring true—then in 1962, and now here again in Loch Sheldrake.

The problems (much like over at *Sweeney Todd*) begin with the set. *A Funny Thing Happened on the Way to the Forum* is sharing a stage with *Children of Eden*. Every show here at Stagedoor must share a theater, and the sets are designed to be moved on and off with ease (between, say, an afternoon performance of *Forum* and an evening performance of *Eden*). If that's not possible, the main backdrop is then designed to work for both shows. Unfortunately, one of the tech staff made an innocent computation error and these two sets didn't work in tandem, nor could they be removed. While the problem is being sorted out, the cast of *A Funny Thing Happened on the Way to the Forum* must rehearse its complicated entrances and exits ducking under, and snaking through, the *Children of Eden* scenery.

"When will we rehearse on *our* set?" one kid asks.

"That's what I'd like to know," *Forum*'s director replies.

Rehearsals have been slow going. The cast had run "Comedy Tonight" to death, and Harry felt the scene was getting less funny each time. Somehow, by smoothing out the transitions—between the Proteans and their spears, between the full-cast kick line that ends the show's opening number—they'd ironed out the funny, too.

During Hell Week, they run through act one, and the choreographer is still tinkering. At this point in the show, Pseudolus, the slave, imagines what his life might be like if he could buy his freedom. He performs a duet—with his master's son—a song called "Free." *"I'll be so conscientious that I may vote twice!"* Pseudolus sings, *"Can you see me? Can you see me?"*

The song builds to a climax:

Pseudolus: *"I'll be Pseudolus, the pillar of society. I'll be Pseudolus the man, if I can only be—"*

Hero: "Free."

Pseudolus: "Sing it!"

Hero: *"Free!"*

Pseudolus: "Spell it!"

Hero: "F-R-double—"

Pseudolus: "No, the long way!"

Hero: "F-R-E-E!"

Both: *"Free!"*

The choreographer has an idea. "You two should play patty-cake," she says, slapping her hands together. "You should play patty-cake on free. *F-R-E-E.*"

Harry, incredulous, raises an eyebrow. "Patty-cake?" he says. The choreographer—perhaps tired of Harry's second-guessing—shrugs. "I'm fine with your ideas," she says. But the director backs her up. "Try it," he says. "It'll be funnier with patty-cake."

Harry boils over. He worries that the show is overchoreographed, leaving little room for him to experiment, to play around, to put his own stamp on the role. In "Pretty Little Picture"—in which he lays out a future of marital bliss for two young lovers—he's instructed to trace a picture frame (in the air) with his fingers every time he sings, *"It's a pretty little picture, oh my! Pretty little picture, how true!"*

"It's too literal," Harry says. He's replaying the show in his mind, overthinking every scene. And it's affecting his performance. Bits of dialogue that used to score big laughs in rehearsal are now reduced to mere throwaway lines.

Harry, meanwhile, is pulled away from rehearsal early in Hell Week for a final costume fitting. *Forum* hasn't been performed at Stagedoor in over a decade. And so Todd Roberts, the head of the costume shop—a man who made his own chaps for a staff costume party—is building the pieces for this show himself, from scratch. The Pseudolus getup, designed with Harry in mind, is a maroon tunic, with mustard-yellow pants and a braided belt. Black Roman sandals and an elastic headband complete the look. The costume is beautifully made. Todd is a perfectionist; he not only designed and executed Harry's Pseudolus costume himself, he'll even dye an undershirt to match. And yet Harry pushes back. He stares at his reflection in the mirror and pulls at the pants. He tugs at the tunic, his face scrunching up.

Excerpts from the conversation in the costume shop:

Harry: [pulling at the tunic] "Can you take this in? It feels too loose. What I do is physical. I'm worried it'll get lost."

Todd: "How physical?"

Harry: [exasperated] "I don't know. Can I just see what it looks like?"

Todd: "Well, I'll have to take in the side, recut it, and then put the sleeve back on. Which is fine . . ."

Harry: "If the costume is tighter, I'll feel pulled together."

Todd: "Honey, if it makes you feel better we'll do it. This is a Todd Roberts original! But don't worry about what *I* want."

Harry: [beat] "Where did you get the material for these pants?"

Todd: "From half the couches in Loch Sheldrake."

And scene.

The hits keep on coming. At rehearsal—the day before Sneak Peek—Harry is surprised to find that the cast of *A Funny Thing Happened on the Way to the Forum* will be doing an act swap with *Into the Woods*. "We'd missed so much rehearsal already," Harry says, "with me being away, with the director being sick. I'm embarrassed to do the show in front of Brian and Charlotte [Maltby] and everyone from *Into the Woods*."

The pressure has caught up with Harry—and it's a much larger issue than simply the costumes or the tragicomic goings on at *A Funny Thing Happened on the Way to the Forum*. "It's the expectations," he says. "This is going to show up on YouTube."

Bingo.

It's a very modern issue, this monkey on the back that Harry and this generation of aspiring performers face. When Harry showed up at the University of Michigan orientation a week ago, not only was he well acquainted with his classmates—they'd been chatting on Facebook since their acceptance letters arrived—but he'd also already seen most of them perform. "Everyone has clips on YouTube," he says. More than that, he'd formed opinions about their talent. How could he not? And he wasn't alone. Harry knew of people who'd already ranked the incoming musical theater freshman classes—across rival programs like the College-Conservatory of Music in Cincinnati, and Elon University in North Carolina—by comparing and debating You-Tube links.

The unique problem facing this generation: Everything is record-ed. There is no longer a safe space to make mistakes, which is perhaps the most essential step to growth. Brent Wagner, the head of Michi-gan's musical theater program, strongly suggests his students remove their YouTube clips, because no one should be judged in the training stage. "Technology can put a scrutiny on your work that is intimidat-ing," he says. "I don't think high school students have a perspective on technology, and what is in their best interest to post. YouTube is what, three years old? We're all at its mercy. We're all learning. But these young people are growing up without a sense of privacy." They don't know what they gave up.

Over lunch at Stagedoor one afternoon, Harry got increasingly de-fensive over a clip from a 2008 camp production of *Guys & Dolls*, in which he sang "Sit Down You're Rockin' the Boat." The quality of the video is grainy, but it's clear to any watcher that Harry is exceptionally talented. Yet he tightens up at the mention of this short clip. Not be-cause he wasn't proud of the show—he was, immensely—but because, if you scroll down, amidst a stream of celebratory plaudits, one snarky commenter on YouTube wrote in: "changing keys = unimpressive." It's true, the music director at Stagedoor had transposed "Sit Down You're Rockin' the Boat" for Harry, so it would fit more comfortably in his range. (This is a no-no on Broadway, where it would cost too much money to reorchestrate a score for a single performer, unless you're such a big star that your name is selling tickets.) But it didn't take away from his talent.

"Everyone is starring in their own *Truman Show*," Harry says, ex-hausted. "When you know someone is filming a performance, you

Harry Katzman as Nicely-Nicely Johnson in a 2008 Stagedoor production of *Guys & Dolls*. Harry was not thrilled to be cast in this role—he felt he'd done it all before—but says it was "good for his résumé." "It's a part I'd like to play again someday." he says. "It fits my *type*."

think, *This is how people are going to remember you doing it.* But that might not be me at my full potential. And that's not what the theater is about. That's why we do theater and not film. Because it's live!"

It's as if these kids are living in a prison of their own digital making. While Stagedoor does its best to curtail the use of cell phones, at home every mistake is tweeted. Every gaffe is caught on video and then broadcast like some twenty-four-hour high school news cycle, with no context. Forget the loss of innocence. Spontaneity is now threatened, too.

These kids are not alone in facing this. While it is not often discussed in the open, YouTube and flipcams are interfering with live performance. It's something Tony-winning talents with names you'd recognize are grappling with right now. And it threatens to change the face of live performance. A well-known Broadway performer tells me,

"You're onstage singing and then you see a little red light in row G on the aisle, and it takes you out of the performance. You think, *Shit, this is going to be on YouTube tonight.* And then you think, *How did I sing that song in act one, and how did I do this?.*"

This wasn't as much of a problem in the old days. In his biography, Sondheim discusses the first preview of any show, saying, "It's always an ordeal. I hated it because all the professional bitches come—and tell their friends how terrible it is." But the bad word could only travel as fast as the telegram. The real problems began with Internet chat rooms, where obsessed theater fans on sites like All That Chat take swipes at performers from the comfort (and anonymity) of their own couch. But suddenly there's a video clip to back up every insane rant on who is the fiercest Elphaba—drawing on camera-phone evidence from *Wicked* companies as far as South Africa. But even the best singers have rough days, where in the face of exhaustion from eight shows a week they miss the high F at the end of "Defying Gravity."

The real problem Harry faces isn't begrudging a friend's success, or that he's somehow late to the party because he isn't a teenage superstar. He needs to get out of his own head. "I want the show to be perfect," he says. "I have this pressure thing, of making it perfect. Everyone has always told me, 'You're perfect for Pseudolus.' But can I pull this off? Will I be funny? I'm onstage and I'm thinking, *Is this over-the-top? Is this too hammy?* What are they going to laugh at?'"

———

Into the Woods rehearsal, Oasis Theater. Act two run-through. The forbidden, adulterous kiss between Cinderella's Prince and the Baker's Wife. "This is not right," the Baker's Wife says. But Cinderella's Prince eases her concerns, taking her hands in his, singing: *"Right and wrong don't matter in the wood, only feelings. Let us meet the moment unblushed. Life is often so unpleasant—you must know that, as a peasant. Best to take the moment present as a present for the moment."*

With that, today the Prince politely kisses her cheek.

Chris Armbrister, the director, in a backwards hat and Hawaiian shirt with pinup girls on it, stops the scene. "Remember," Chris says, "the kiss is supposed to be *passionate*. The Baker's Wife is married. The Prince has to tempt her to cheat." They run it again, but the scene repeats itself beat-for-beat, with yet another polite peck on the cheek.

On the next go, the Baker's Wife takes matters into her own hands, grabbing Cinderella's Prince and jamming her tongue down his throat for all to see. Brian Muller—dressed in a gray T-shirt, one leg of his sweatpants rolled up—is watching from the seats, and shouts: "That's awkward!" Unsure of how to react, the Prince simply puts out his hands palms up, as if to say, "It wasn't me!"

Fatigue has set in. And if the cast of *Into the Woods* is suffering from low energy at this Hell Week rehearsal, well, so be it. The Wolf is in the infirmary, contending with a fever. (When he returns to the show, he's lost so much weight he needs to hold his pants up with one paw.) Cinderella was just discharged from an overnight stay at the infirmary, and while she's been cleared for rehearsal, she's still wearing a VOCAL REST sticker. Little Red is on vocal rest, too. Which doesn't mean she's off her game. True to the precocious nature of that character, when Brian misses a line during a run-through of the prologue, Little Red points an accusatory finger at him.

Into the Woods clocks in at close to three hours, and the cast has yet to complete a single full run-through. The goal today, Tuesday of this final week, is to plow through without stopping. But when one actress steps out of a scene to ask a question, and then another follows suit, the momentum dissolves. The director looks over at Brian and Leah Fishbaugh (the actress playing the Baker's Wife), displeased. They're holding their "newborn baby" sloppily, and the director shouts: "I don't want to see the top of the baby's *plastic head*, please."

The problems continue. There is a very distinct difference in tone between act one and act two of *Into the Woods*. The first half is a fairy tale in which the forest is a place of wonder. But after intermission, the Giant shows up, and the forest becomes a dangerous place where the beast's errant footfall can kill. Cinderella, her Prince, the Baker, and Little Red all head back into the now-precarious woods, and here in the Oasis Theater the actors circle the stage, peering around, singing:

Jack: *"Into the woods to slay the giant."*

Baker's Wife: *"Into the woods to shield the child."*

Little Red: *"To flee the winds . . ."*

Baker: *"To find a future . . ."*

The director stops the parade, interjecting: "The woods are a dangerous place, and it looks like you're all shopping for groceries."

Brian wipes his forehead, his shoulders slouching in on themselves. The Baker, a beta male struggling with forces beyond his control, was a different role for him. It's easy for a confident teenager to play the aggressor—to bark instructions, to be worshipped. "We talk about characters as having A status or B status," Brian says. "The A status character is dominant. I can play A status." This is different. In act two of *Into the Woods*, the angry Giant, busy searching for the boy who stole his harp and his beloved golden goose, kills the Baker's Wife. Suddenly, the Baker—a man terrified of parenthood—is left a single father to a defenseless baby.

Brian had the script memorized; he could be seen walking around camp shouting his lines at people passing by. But he was struggling with the climax of act two, when in the wake of this death, the Baker comes to recognize just how difficult and complicated and awful life can be. At his wit's end, he abandons his infant son to Cinderella— saying the child will have a better life in the care of a princess than with a baker.

But the Baker does not get very far before his own long-absent and mysterious father suddenly appears. "Trouble is, son, the farther you run, the more you feel undefined," he says, "for what you have left undone, and more, what you have left behind."

Into the Woods is a show about taking responsibility, about growing up. At eighteen, was Brian out of his emotional depth? Where would this character come from?

———

Sometimes, it was hard to believe Brian Muller—intelligent, square-jawed, well mannered—had ever had a bad day in his life. He'd been charmed, stumbling into theater camp by chance and finding out he was not just a good actor, but *preternaturally* good. He'd been accepted to the acclaimed program at Carnegie Mellon, a coup, but deferred when a role in an Equity national tour fell in his lap.

Though it seems unlikely now, impossible even, Brian—a hair shy of six feet tall—had once been the smallest kid in his class. Being an adorable twelve-year-old had its advantages, but the novelty wears off. "As a freshman in high school," Brian says, "I was maybe five feet tall."

"I was worried when he first went to camp," his mother says, "because he was so small. He was always small."

Puberty never arrives on schedule. But at some point, Brian's parents had to admit, the boy should be growing by now, shouldn't he? Experts were consulted, followed by research, disagreements, and consultations.

Brian, full head shorter than his classmates, still played on the basketball team, but he knew the floor was no longer equal. Which was the least of his problems, truth be told. Teenagers are often betrayed by their bodies, with overactive hormones wreaking havoc on their skin, playing fast and loose with their emotions. But the only thing worse than going through puberty is *not* going through it. That you and your friends are experiencing that hell together is the only thing that makes the ordeal bearable.

Brian Muller played George Gibbs in a production of *Our Town*, following his fresh-man year in high school. He considers this production a turning point in his life, helping him decide to pursue acting as a profession.

For Brian, whose shoulders at fifteen didn't yet square, whose voice hadn't yet dropped, the impact was emotional as much as it was physical. "I'd go to parties," Brian says, "and I'd be mistaken for a middle school kid." He was an otherwise well-adjusted, even-tempered kid forced to confront a lesson head-on, feeling anger maybe for the first time.

In time, Brian's body caught up with those of his peers. Brian never had a growth spurt per se. He never woke up a man in boy's clothing. His development was more deliberate, a slow burn. And he was once again comfortably part of the majority. But it was an experience— a rejection, a sense of alienation—to draw on. It was a tool in an actor's arsenal.

Standing in rehearsal for *Into the Woods*, alone on the bare stage during Hell Week, Brian was preparing to sing through "No More"—the show's climax.

"*No more questions, please. No more tests,*" Brian sings. "*Comes the day you say 'What for?' Please—no more.*"

The Baker is throwing up his hands. There was just a handful of his fellow actors seated in the audience that afternoon, but everyone in the room fell silent. The actress playing the Baker's Wife knew what she'd seen, and broke down in tears. It was a stunning performance.

What changed?

"I was staring at the baby," Brian says, "and I was just angry. The character was angry at the world, angry at what happened, angry at himself. And it clicked."

CHAPTER 8

Performance Weekend

8 A.M. SATURDAY.

She knew before she opened her eyes. It was Saturday morning, the day of her final Stagedoor Manor performance, and Rachael Singer could barely breathe. She could feel it in her throat—a tightening— and a full-blown panic set in. Her friends and roommates asked what they could do to help; Rachael sent them downstairs to fetch her breakfast and they returned with seven different kinds of cereal. "We didn't know what you wanted," one girl said. "So we got you all of them." Rachael took one look at the haul and turned her head away. The variety wasn't the problem. She was feeling so sick that even the sight of Special K made her nauseous.

Rachael forced herself into the shower. She tried to make a sound, to sing a note. But nothing came. Three weeks of hard work. For what? She eased into a pair of sweatpants and a gray Emerson hooded sweatshirt—she was moving so slowly—and a counselor walked her over to the infirmary.

Nearly this same scene had played out the day before. Rachael woke up on Friday with a sore throat. She tried to ignore it, and gamely struggled through her first official performance of *Sweeney Todd*— worrying less about her parents in the audience or the scenery changes (which had been ironed out somewhat in the twenty-four hours since the dress rehearsal) than about just making it through to the curtain call. Rachael had been so preoccupied with hitting her marks that she barely noticed the talent scouts from the Macy's Thanksgiving Day Parade, who were passing through Stagedoor that day in search of a squeaky-clean act for a new float; instead, at *Sweeney Todd* they found children with fake blood dripping from their mouths. "Still, we were trying to look perky!" one girl says.

Rachael took her bow on Friday afternoon and walked directly from the Elsie Theater stage to the infirmary. The nurse took her temperature: 103 degrees. She put the girl on a round of antibiotics, plus the anti-inflammatory drug prednisone, then hooked her up to a nebulizer—a miracle machine typically used by asthmatics to shoot medicine directly into the lungs. It was a high-tech treatment plan for a summer camp, and a course of action Rachael prayed might do the trick (despite all evidence to the contrary). As she sat in the infirmary, Rachael's thoughts turned from self-preservation to the task at hand: Saturday evening's performance of *Sweeney Todd*. "What if I can't go on?" Rachael said to herself, allowing her mind to go to that terrible place for the first time.

While Rachael was resting on Saturday morning, while her friends were fetching cereal for her, a rumor spread through the dining hall: Rachael was sick, and if she didn't recover, the director of *Sweeney Todd* had asked Natalie Walker to go on in her place. The rumor turned out to be not so much wrong as premature: it wasn't until *after* breakfast that Jeff Murphy tracked Natalie down. A closed-door meeting was convened in the camp's main office. It was too soon to tell if Rachael would be able to perform, the nurse had told Jeff. She still had another dose of prednisone to take, and of course that might help, but Jeff had the show to think about.

"If Rachael can't go on," he asked Natalie, "will *you* do it?"

Natalie ran her hands through her long dark hair, and pouted. "I'm nervous," she said. Still, she had to admit, it would be quite a send-off, stepping in for Mrs. Lovett at the last minute. Plus, she hadn't really been given the chance to show off much that session. She'd been cast as Desirée Armfeldt in *A Little Night Music*. And while Desirée is a lead role (that show is ostensibly about her romance with Fredrik), she sings just one song. And that song is "Send in the Clowns," written originally with the actress Glynis Johns (and her inability to sustain a note) in mind. That's why every line ends with a short note. "Isn't it rich? Are we a pair?" One can't really belt *rich*. It's a gorgeous piece. But no one ever leaves the theater thinking, "Wow, that actress really talked the *shit* out of that song."

Natalie, her eyes blinking dramatically the way they do when she's lost in thought, considered Jeff's request and finally issued her reply: "I had a dream two nights ago that I went on as Mrs. Lovett." A rehearsal was arranged, tentatively, for 4 P.M. on Saturday afternoon. Natalie could play Desirée Armfeldt at 1:30 P.M. in the camp's Oasis Theater, and still tie on Mrs. Lovett's apron for a 7:30 P.M. curtain in the Elsie.

The director was relieved, of course. And terribly nervous for Rachael, adorable as she rested in the infirmary, draped in her favorite sweatshirt. Still, when he relayed this anecdote—about Natalie's prescient dream—to some of the camp's artistic staff just minutes later, these catty men couldn't help but unleash a barrage of *All About Eve* jokes, citing the original scheming understudy. "You know Natalie doesn't even *need* that script," one director laughed. It wasn't true. But far be it for a member of the artistic staff to pass up a chance to make an Eve Harrington reference.

12:30 P.M. LUNCH.

After several hours in the infirmary, Rachael mustered the strength to return to her room temporarily, shower again (the hot water always made her feel better), and get some tea from the cafeteria. On her walk back she passed Harry Katzman, who gave her a hug and some words of encouragement, though Harry's mind admittedly was elsewhere. At that moment, a voice came over the camp loudspeaker: "Would the cast of *A Funny Thing Happened on the Way to the Forum* please report to the Camelot courtyard for a meeting?"

Harry, dressed in rolled-up jeans, his sunglasses hanging from his polo shirt, rubbed his face (already flushed) with both hands. He looked up at the sky. A comically large black cloud—like something out of a *Peanuts* cartoon strip—was rolling in. The disappointment was written all over Harry's face. What would become of his show, which was scheduled to play the camp's outdoor Forum Theater that night?

Harry Katzman—the actor consumed with fear of imperfection, of his lesser work being made public on YouTube—was about to discover just how little control he actually had over this show.

The *Forum* cast assembled in the courtyard as directed, and the show's stage manager confirmed what even the youngest kids already guessed at: "We're going to a rain schedule." The Saturday evening performance (Harry's last at Stagedoor) would now be performed in the Playhouse, at the decidedly less glamorous time of 5 P.M. Harry shook his head and let out a sigh. The camp owner, Cindy Samuelson, tried to put a positive spin on the last-minute venue change. "It's a good thing!" she said. "More people will get to see the show!" If nothing else, that was certainly true: Stagedoor Manor matinees are at 1:30 P.M. Evening performances at 7:30 P.M. At 5 P.M. *Forum* would have nothing to compete with but the steak-and-eggs at the Liberty Diner.

Harry's friends would get in to see the show. But would it be any good? *A Funny Thing Happened on the Way to the Forum* is a farce—with entrances and exits piled on top of one another. For two and a half weeks, Harry had massaged those scenes, those songs, to play in the camp's intimate Forum Theater. Now what? Comedies are nothing if not delicate. Plus, Harry's Pseudolus was mischievous, and at the Forum he was never more than a few feet from the front row of seats. He could easily come out into the audience and play off the parents. That simply wouldn't be possible at the Playhouse—a 300-seat standard proscenium where the front row is ten feet from the stage.

Harry took a deep breath. Perhaps the rain was just that thing Orson Welles used to talk about, that *bad thing*, he sometimes called it. The legendary artist—extremely superstitious, known to be afraid of *numbers*—was unsure of a production's potential success until something went spectacularly wrong before opening night. In rehearsal, he'd look for it, pray for it. He needed it. Maybe the rain was just Harry's bad thing.

Or maybe not. "The Playhouse is a barn," Harry says, dramatically. "It echoes. Dialogue lingers. And comedy gets lost. I've heard of shows being moved inside before." Dramatic pause. "But this is a nightmare."

1:30 P.M.

When the curtain went up on *A Little Night Music* that afternoon, when Natalie Walker emerged onstage as Desirée Armfeldt dressed in a Marie Antoinette–style gown and towering wig, Rachael Singer was quarantined in the infirmary with her parents, who'd flown in from Florida for their daughter's final performance at Stagedoor Manor, the end of a successful and happy four-summer run. They were relieved to find that Rachael's throat strain had eased by the afternoon; she could now carry on a conversation, could now be heard above a whisper. Unfortunately, their daughter was still shaky on her feet, in part from the fever still working its way through her system. In the shower, Rachael warmed up her voice, but to mixed results. She'd never go on that evening, she felt, and the tears welled up in her eyes.

Meanwhile, if Natalie hadn't entirely wanted to step in for Rachael before, something would happen to change her mind. For two hours, Natalie performed beautifully in *A Little Night Music*—you could almost forget she was probably thirty years too young for the role of Desirée, the aging actress at the show's center. And it's a testament to her skill (and Raymond Zilberberg's direction) that at eighteen years old Natalie was able to find the humanity in the role of an absent single mother who seduces two married men and *still* manages to play the victim.

Unfortunately, with thirty seconds left in Natalie's climactic second-act number, "Send in the Clowns"—with Fredrik onstage rejecting her advances, with the tears welling up inside of her—Natalie takes a deep breath, and sings, *"But where are the clowns? Quick send in the clowns. Don't bother* [pause] *they're—"*

And then the fire alarm went off.

The show's smoke effect was to blame, not that it matters. Because the damage was done. A garish strobe light flickered on, coupled with a deafening and shrill noise. Younger siblings put their hands up to their ears, shielding their delicate eardrums from the awful sound. Natalie, for her part, let out a laugh. When the siren finally cut off—after an impossibly long minute—she finished the song, and the audience applauded, both for her assured performance and her grace under fire (alarm). But backstage, Natalie couldn't help but cry. "I'm devastated," she says. "This was the last song I'm ever going to sing at Stagedoor."

Natalie Walker appears as the actress Desirée Armfeldt in *A Little Night Music*—part of the camp's 2009 Sondheim festival.

Unless, of course, Rachael couldn't go on.

As instructed, Natalie collected her belongings, left her wig cap in place, and found the music director of *Sweeney Todd* to run through the score. It was 4 P.M. In a little over three hours, *Sweeney Todd* would go up at the Elsie Theater. But who would play Mrs. Lovett was still very much in doubt.

4 P.M.

The cast of *West Side Story* finishes their matinee at the Playhouse, and the Stagedoor Manor tech crew immediately begins the arduous process of loading out that show's elaborate set—Maria's balcony, the drugstore—and loading in the flats for *A Funny Thing Happened on the Way to the Forum*'s 5 P.M. curtain. It turns out the changeover takes longer than anticipated. The upshot: Harry Katzman and the company of *Forum* are now able to at least take a stab at running through act two's chase sequence in this new and unfamiliar space.

At 6 P.M., Harry—dressed in Pseudolus's maroon tunic—takes his place onstage for the show, a full hour behind schedule, the anticipation only building. He can hear the director out front, greeting the parents, cracking, "Welcome to the newly built *Forum* stage."

And just like that the overture begins.

From the first measure of "Comedy Tonight" it's obvious just how much the surprise change in venue has messed with the rhythm of the show. Previously, outside at the Forum Theater, Harry had practiced jumping into the audience on certain lyrics in the opening number. He planned on sidling up to someone's weirdo relative and pointing, "something familiar, *something peculiar.*" At the performance for parents on Friday afternoon, the joke got a huge laugh. But tonight, at the Playhouse, it flatlines. It just looks like Harry is pointing into the blackness of the theater, and the motion is greeted with dead air. Sensing the disaster that is "Comedy Tonight," Harry starts to speed up, swallowing lyrics in the process. When he shouts "Open up the curtain!" the red drapes slowly creak apart.

The applause for "Comedy Tonight" is the worst kind: polite.

Standing safely offstage just after this opening number, Harry wipes some flop sweat from his brow and adjusts his headband. Theater performers often talk about the thrill of doing a musical. It's like a bullet leaving a gun's chamber: once the overture begins, the show's impossible to stop and, for better or worse, you better run with it. "But I wanted to cry," Harry says. "The staging deteriorated." What to do? Harry—the one afraid of making a mistake, lest it wind up broadcast on the Internet—remembered a cardinal rule: There are no excuses in the theater. And so he started to improvise, throwing everything at the wall, recalibrating his gestures, his glances, to the new space. He went bigger, and why not? There's a reason all three men who played Pseudolus on Broadway over the years won Tony Awards for it. Who did the role best is a matter of how you like your ham cooked.

And Harry's only getting started. Early in the show, Pseudolus is accused of "parading" as a citizen. "Believe me, master," Pseudolus states, "I was not *parading*." With that, Harry throws his left hand in the air and does an exaggerated jaunt across the stage. [beat] "*This* is parading." The cast can barely keep it together.

Pseudolus soon agrees to help his owner's son pursue his true love—a courtesan in the House of Marcus Lycus. To lure this woman out of the brothel, Pseudolus asks to preview this man's *wares*. Onstage, Harry reclines on a chaise lounge as the inventory of women is presented to him, one by one. Gymnasia, he's told, is "a giant stage on which a thousand dramas can be played." The young girl emerges cracking a whip, and Harry takes that as his cue. He drops to the floor,

Longtime friends Harry Katzman and Ben Blackman display true chemistry in *A Funny Thing Happened on the Way to the Forum* at Stagedoor Manor.

lying on his back with his feet up in the air, pawing at the whip like a cat playing with a piece of yarn. Harry pants. He swats at the whip again. He throws in a girlish giggle.

When Vibrata, "exotic as a desert bloom, wondrous as a flamingo, lithe as a tigress," appears, Harry snuggles up to her breast before taking her measurements. "She may be the right length," Harry says, "but is it right for *me*?" He stands back-to-back with her. "How often would we find ourselves in this position? Or *this* position? Or *this*?" Harry suddenly picks the girl up and hugs her; he turns her around and grabs her from behind. "Or *this* position! Or *this*!" The actress looks surprised, but goes with it—and is rewarded with shouts of approval.

In the opening number tonight, Harry—so spooked by the stage—was asking for laughs. And when an actor asks for laughs, they never come. Harry knew that. He just needed a reminder.

But there is something more impressive happening onstage: Harry (the Zero Mostel of Stagedoor Manor) is suddenly generous with his co-stars. When a fellow actor earns a laugh, Harry steps out of the way and happily lets them enjoy the moment. One of Harry's best friends, Ben Blackman, was cast as Hysterium—the head eunuch—and his well-tuned comic timing is on perfect display tonight, his performance only enhanced by an endearing (if slight) speech impediment. Instead of beckoning for Hero, Ben shouts for *"He-wo!"*

In rehearsal, Harry had struggled with the pressure of leading this cast. But now he saw the way to succeed together, to play off of each other. In act two, Pseudolus and Hysterium duet on the song "Lovely." For Pseudolus's plan to work—to spirit away the lovers in secret—he has to convince Hysterium to masquerade as a courtesan. More than simply putting on a dress, he desperately needs Hysterium to play a convincing woman. In short, he needs Hysterium to feel *pretty*.

"He'll never believe I'm a girl," Hysterium cries. "Look at me. Just look at me!"

And so Harry—suddenly the straight man—begins to sing, earnestly showering his friend with lavish praise: *"You're lovely. Absolutely lovely. Who'd believe the loveliness of you. Perfect, sweet and warm and winsome, radiant as in some dream come true."*

Ben warms up, and mines the comedy from the situation—demanding jewelry! and flowers! to complete his Sapphic transformation. Harry steps back, reveling in Ben's triumph.

"I'm lovely," Ben sings, *"Absolutely lovely. Who'd believe the loveliness of me?"*

With ten minutes left in the show, there's a rare moment of calm for Pseudolus, who is otherwise in nearly every scene. Harry stands at the back of the Playhouse, sweating through a quick costume change. And for him, time suddenly stands still, and he's able to take the enormity of the scene in. The parents in their seats. His friends onstage. The roar of laughter rolling through the Playhouse.

It has been an arduous path to this point in his life. "I've been through more than a lot of people my age," Harry says, preferring to let the comment sit there, rather than wallow. Ask Harry about his childhood in London, about surviving his teenage years on two continents, about his application to Michigan, and the same phrase comes up: "I never thought I was what people were looking for." Four years ago, Harry arrived at camp with a (some might say) obnoxious level of bravado. He was so eager to fit in, he overcompensated. But over the next four years, the true joy was watching him learn to drop the act. To lose the armor. He could be himself, and not a *caricature* of himself. Watching Harry shine in *The Mystery of Edwin Drood*? Or in *A Funny Thing Happened on the Way to the Forum*? For the staff at camp, that was just gravy.

"Graduating from Stagedoor means more to me than graduating from high school," Harry says. These people accepted him when he didn't accept himself, when he was more comfortable seated in a West

End theater full of strangers than in his own skin. That feeling of not being good enough never really goes away. (What artist isn't fighting the undertow?) But Harry has learned there was something he could do about it. He could work harder. He could prepare himself so that when the rejections come (and they come for everyone) he'll know he's done all he could. "A lot of my friends," Harry says, "when they don't get a job, they think: *It's not me, it's them. It's the casting director. It's the producer. It's their problem.* But I don't think that's it. Sometimes it *is* you. You need more training. You need more experience." His parents didn't have to worry about Harry dropping out of school and trading his dorm room for a Manhattan sublet. Harry had reconciled his ambitions. Stagedoor Manor confirmed that he had the talent to succeed beyond his high school drama program. His camp friends inspired him, showing him what was possible in New York. But Harry would succeed on his own timetable.

And just like that, Harry is right back in the show. "Release that man!" he shouts from the back of the Playhouse, charging through the aisle and leaping up onto the stage. When the show is over, he takes his bow, throws on his jeans backstage, and in the pouring rain he runs to the Elsie Theater. He is proud of his performance in *A Funny Thing Happened on the Way to the Forum*, of what he pulled off in this short time. There would be time to reflect further, but for now he had to know: What happened to Rachael Singer?

6 P.M.

Rachael pulls herself up by the bootstraps of her character shoes and makes her way over to the camp's makeup studio. The nurse had taken her temperature one last time, had administered the final dose of steroid. The staff was not happy to let her go, not at all sure that this was the wise move. Watching his daughter leave the infirmary, Mike

Singer wasn't convinced she'd make it to the stage, or that he was even right to let her try.

Rachael sits down in front of the mirror and squints, her face bathed in the harsh light of a dozen or so round bulbs. She ties her hair up in a bun and tries to smile. There is a line of twenty-five kids waiting behind her—the casts of *Into the Woods*, *The Who's Tommy*, and *The Children's Hour* among them. The makeup artist applies foundation first, then a little rouge to warm up her face. Rachael doesn't say much as she puts on her wig cap, fastening Mrs. Lovett's funny red hair into place. She looks herself over. The wig still looks silly, she thinks, like a homeless Raggedy Ann.

Rachael hugs her body tight and wonders out loud whether she'll have the strength—or the voice—to perform. In the minutes before the doors open to the Elsie Theater on Saturday evening, she leans against the piano, more for balance than anything, and attempts to sing through the first bars of "The Worst Pies in London."

"You can screech through it," says the director, Jeff Murphy.

"Push it out," the music director says. "You have the notes." But Rachael cuts the warm-up short. Natalie Walker looks on, waiting in the wings, not wanting to make her friend uncomfortable, but ready to perform if need be.

No one in the audience knew for sure who would walk out onstage as Mrs. Lovett; the character isn't in the show's opening number. As if the prologue were written specifically to add suspense to this performance tonight, Sweeney Todd sings: *What happened then—well, that's the play, and he wouldn't want us to give it away.*

Blackout. The cast exits the stage. Mrs. Lovett's pie shop is wheeled out. A woman in a red wig emerges with a rolling pin in hand.

"A customer!" she shrieks.

Lights up on Rachael Singer, smiling broadly, beneath that hideous wig—to deafening applause.

But the thrill of seeing this girl shine is quickly dashed. Halfway through "The Worst Pies In London," her voice gives out. Rachael drops the melody a full octave, growling: *Mrs. Mooney has a pie shop, does a business but I notice something weird. Lately all her neighbors' cats have disappeared.*" Rachael's father, seated out front, fears his daughter might walk off the stage at the end of this number and not return. He is right to be concerned. "You know when you feel really sick," Rachael says later, "and your body gets hot and you feel like you might pass out? That's how I felt. I couldn't even think of what words were coming next."

Mrs. Lovett has a difficult first act; "The Worst Pies in London" transitions directly into "Poor Thing." In rehearsal, even in good health, Rachael had struggled with the lyrics—not just with spitting them out, but with their meaning. For three weeks the director had encouraged Rachael to make choices. He'd given her a copy of the video of Angela Lansbury in *Sweeney Todd*, hoping she might be inspired. For Rachael, a breakthrough came, finally. But it had nothing to do with the DVD.

Tonight, with her voice taken from her, Rachael needs to rely on another instrument: her body. She does not walk offstage, as her father feared. Instead she makes smart, bold acting choices to get through the next two hours. On her pie shop counter, Rachael installs a ceramic mug of water, a prop she returns to often to revive her voice; after each sip, she lets out a big Cockney sigh of relief, an obnoxious "*aaaaahh.*" It begins to get laughs—the good kind—adding a level of crazy to this character.

In "Poor Thing," Rachael is teasing Sweeney Todd. "You poor thing," she says caressing this man, pronouncing *poor* like *paw*. "You *paw paw paw paw* thing." When the Beggar Woman appears—singing her signature refrain, *"Alms! Alms! For a miserable woman"*—Rachael mocks her, mimicking, *"Alms! Alms!"* Where are these ideas coming from? Every syllable is drawn out. Every gesture exaggerated. When

Mrs. Lovett realizes, at the end of act one, that Sweeney Todd killed Signor Pirelli, Rachael says, almost flirtatiously: "Mr. *Teeeeeeeee*. You didn't!"

Rachael's energy is flagging—offstage she bites into a candy bar for a boost—but she uses the fatigue to her advantage. Walking up the stairs to Sweeney Todd's barbershop, she holds on to the railing and says, "My knees aren't what they used to be." Acting is being authentic in inauthentic situations. And Rachael nails that tonight: she isn't merely reciting memorized lines, she is in the moment, reacting to what is directly in front of her. And it makes all the difference.

Hugh Wheeler, who wrote the book for *Sweeney Todd,* once addressed the difficulty in showcasing this modern American opera about a murderous barber and a woman who bakes flesh pies: "The hardest thing of all was how to take these two really disgusting people and write them in such a way that the audience can rather love them." Tonight, the audience loves Mrs. Lovett, a woman with few redeeming qualities, because Rachael makes her a pathetic character. But a pathetic character whose motivations we can understand. This grotesque woman is so lonely, so in love with Sweeney Todd that she'd happily dispose of dead bodies to remain in his life. And the audience sympathizes with her despite her unconscionable actions. It may be absurd for an eighteen-year-old to be cast as Mrs. Lovett, but she's a woman these love-starved teenagers can more than relate to.

In the end, Natalie wouldn't need to go on. She watched act two from backstage—because Rachael asked her to stay, because Rachael needed the reassurance of a friend waiting in the wings. But halfway through the second act, Natalie packs up her things. She scrawls out a note to her friend, "I'm so proud of you," and pins it to the Styrofoam head where Rachael will later stow her wig. Natalie knows this girl won't quit now.

What made Rachael get up out of bed finally? What made the nice girl from Florida, the one who was supposedly content to play short

Jewish girls for the rest of her life, push herself out onstage for that final night at Stagedoor Manor?

It was simple, Rachael says: "I'm not going out like that."

9:30 P.M.

There's something beautifully perverse about a theater camp production of *Into the Woods*. In short, parents will have paid a princely sum for their teenagers to put on a show where everything that goes wrong for these characters is the fault of an overprotective parent. Little Red Ridinghood, Cinderella, Jack—each comes alive here only *after* separating from their parents. (It's a common theme for Sondheim. In *Gypsy*, Mama Rose sings *"Mama's gotta let go!"* Cinderella in *Into the Woods* sings to Little Red Ridinghood, "Mother cannot guide you." Same sentiment, different scrim.)

Believe it or not, tonight's performance of *Into the Woods* at Stagedoor Manor is more successful—on an emotional level—than the original Broadway company. Critics of Sondheim's *Into the Woods* complain that the audience can't possibly care about the fate of Cinderella, Jack, and the Baker, because these characters come onstage so quickly that no single entity has a chance to register. By the time act two rolls around, the audience simply doesn't care about their crises of consciousness. (In 1987, *Into the Woods* lost the best musical Tony Award to *Phantom of the Opera*. Not because it was a better show, necessarily, but because it was clear who to root for.)

The Stagedoor Manor production of *Into the Woods* didn't suffer from any of the character development issues that may have plagued the Broadway production. And here's why: Almost everyone in the standing-room-only audience at the Oasis Theater had watched Brian Muller grow up, from a four-foot-seven grade school kid in *Barnum* eight summers ago—the tyke who lost his voice on the day of the show but managed to sing his heart out anyway—to the striking, upstanding

young man before their eyes tonight. Cindy and Debra Samuelson—
Carl and Elsie's daughters—made sure to be in the audience. Could
this really be the same Brian who, at age eleven, used to sleepwalk so
often they had to install bells on his door so the counselors could hear
him stepping out? "All of a sudden he's this full-grown man," Debra
says, "and this wonderful performer."

Good as Brian was in *Into the Woods* tonight, the emotional connection with the audience had been established long before the curtain went up. His job was simply to nurture it.

And he does, beautifully. In act two, having delivered to the witch
"the cow as white as milk, the cape as red as blood, the hair as yellow
as corn, and the slipper as pure as gold," the Baker and his wife are
rewarded with a child. But the joy is short-lived.

"Opportunity is not a lengthy visitor," Cinderella says.

The Baker is now a single father. Who is to blame? Never sure he
was ready to be a father to begin with, the Baker gives in to the impulse
to abandon all responsibilities, leaving his child with Cinderella and
running off into the woods.

Brian stands on a largely bare stage, just the shadows of the trees
on his face. He's dressed in a heavy coat, having shed his white baker's
hat for something that might protect him in the woods. He runs, but
does not get very far. He has lost more than anyone else onstage, but
he's grown the most. He sings: *"How do you ignore all the witches, all
the curses, all the wolves, all the lies, the false hopes, the goodbyes, the
reverses, all the wondering what even worse is still in store?"*

In Sondheim's *Merrily We Roll Along* (a show about a jaded
film producer looking back on his life), the characters mourn the
loss of innocence. But here it's embraced. The characters in *Into the
Woods* are no longer blindly happy; what's still in store may be worse,
but won't the ride—the delicious and frightening unknown—be
thrilling?

In a few short weeks, Brian will begin rehearsals for the national tour of *Little House on the Prairie*. He deferred his spot at Carnegie Mellon, a very adult decision, to meet the challenges of his first professional job head-on, unsure of what awaits but confident he is prepared to join a company of seasoned performers with Broadway credits, not just as an actor, but as a man. He has grown up. Could there have been a better show for Brian's good-bye than *Into the Woods*?

As the Baker says: "You'll have to take care of yourself now, Jack. It's time."

Brian Muller (as the Baker) advises Little Red Ridinghood (Katherine Leigh Doherty) in *Into the Woods*. This was Brian's sixteenth (and final) show at Stagedoor Manor.

Epilogue

BRIAN MULLER LOOKED EXHAUSTED, HIS EYES TIRED, HIS POS-
ture strained, as he came out from the dressing room after the show
to greet his family and friends. He kissed his mother and father hello.
Jennifer Rudin, then the director of casting and talent development
for Disney Theatrical Productions, had been impressed by Brian's
layered performance and wanted to meet him. Richard Maltby, Jr.—a
Tony winner for *Ain't Misbehavin'*, whose daughter Charlotte played
the Witch in *Into the Woods*—stole a moment from Brian, too. "He
asked me if I knew, in my mind, that this was my last performance at
Stagedoor," Brian recalls. "He said he could tell that this night was
special."

And it was, for endless reasons, but most immediately because it
was the last time these friends would perform onstage together. At
11:30 P.M. Brian, Harry, Rachael, and the members of the Our Time
Cabaret assembled in the dressing room at the Playhouse Theater—in
their reds, whites, and blacks, the colors Jack Romano chose for the
cabaret troupe almost thirty years ago. These cabaret members never

knew Jack (some hadn't even been born when he passed away) but they paid homage to him, to the world he helped create for them. At the end of the cabaret performance, they kneel down and knock on the stage three times—*knock! knock! knock!*—kissing their knuckles, and then throwing their hand into the air. "That was Jack's thing," says Konnie. "Knocking on the stage three times." That's how you knew you did something right. Jack would knock his knuckles on the stage. When the kids do it now, Konnie says, "they're sending their love up to heaven."

Rachael's voice was shot, she knew that. She'd left blood on the

Rachael Singer and Jordan Firstman in a triumphant performance of *Sweeney Todd* in the Elsie Theater. Rachael nearly missed the show due to illness, but pulled herself out of bed, saying: "I'm not going out like that."

stage of the Elsie Theater just an hour ago—her Mrs. Lovett a triumph of determination over health—but refused to miss this last performance of the cabaret. "I gave up my solos," she says. "I'll lip-synch the show, but I'll still get to dance." Which she did, the adrenaline carrying her through.

The Our Time Cabaret revue didn't end until after midnight, with a wave of applause that threatened the structural integrity of the Playhouse. Outside in the brisk air, waiting for his daughter to appear, Rachael's father brushed tears out of his eyes. It was the culmination of so many things—his daughter's four years at Stagedoor, the impossible truth that she'd be heading off to college in a few weeks. "It was all of that," Mike says. When Rachael sings, sometimes he still sees that little girl seated in the backseat of the car, singing along to the Beatles. "This has been a journey for us, too," he says.

The Stagedoor Manor awards ceremony began shortly after 1 A.M. The youngest campers, some just ten years old, were escorted down to the Playhouse. Harry, Brian, and Rachael paraded in alongside their friends—all eighteen graduating seniors, all dressed in red graduation robes. Each was given a chance to make a short speech, the impossible task of reducing a life-affirming experience to a few breaths. "I was born in England," Harry told the younger campers, who hung on his every word. "I moved to South Carolina when I was fourteen. I was the Jew at the Episcopal school. I didn't know if there was any place for me." Rachael talked about the friendships she'd made over the years. Natalie thanked the camp for letting her return this summer. Cindy was onstage, pulling numbers from a hat, the order of speakers drawn at random. But it seemed appropriate that she pulled Brian's name last. He'd been there the longest, was one of the only campers left who'd met her father, and really, he'd grown up at Stagedoor in every sense.

"I've been here for eight years," Brian says. "I've done sixteen shows. When I came here, I was this tall." He held his hand out at his waist, like that marker at an amusement park that measures whether a child can safely ride the roller coaster. "Now I'm this tall. This place has changed my life. I had no idea what the next eight years would have in store for me."

And just when one suspected he might get wistful, Brian publicly apologized for chipping his friend and roommate Ben Blackman's tooth on the camp Ping-Pong table when they were seventeen.

"I wish they had Stagedoor for adults," says the singer and actress Mandy Moore. "That would be wildly successful."

I know what she means.

The morning after the Our Time Cabaret performance—the final morning of the session—I had breakfast in the cafeteria with Harry, Rachael, Brian, and a handful of their friends. They were red-eyed but hungry, tearing through single-serving bowls of Apple Jacks like the younger selves they were when they first showed up at camp years ago. At some point a fistful of black Sharpie markers appeared, and we all went downstairs to the Oasis Theater, where twelve hours before Brian played the Baker. At some earlier time, these kids scrawled their names (and their entire Stagedoor Manor résumés) on the wall in a backstage dressing room. Brian's footprint is large: *Tintypes. Barnum. Big River* (original Stagedoor Manor company). *Avenue Q* (original Stagedoor Manor company). *Dark of the Moon. Guys & Dolls*, to name a few. This morning, he proudly added *Into the Woods*.

I was tempted to scrawl my own name up on the wall. I hadn't appeared in a show, but I had lived through a session at Stagedoor Manor, a rare and special gift. Ellen Kleiner, who has worked in the camp office for more than fifteen years, often describes the people who pass through these walls as being one of two types: there are people who work at Stagedoor, she says, and then there are Stagedoor people. "If you asked me to tell you the definition of a Stagedoor person," Ellen says. "I don't know that I could."

After packing up my belongings, I took a final tour of the place, trying to figure out what she meant. I passed through the costume shop. Through the lobby. Past the Jack Romano Playhouse. And as I walked, stories flooded my brain, stories of the people who'd passed through these halls, who'd left a part of themselves on these stages as every actor does.

Jennifer Jason Leigh scored her first professional credit at age nine, opposite Jason Robards in the film *Death of a Stranger,* and since then, in projects as varied as *Fast Times at Ridgemont High* and *Road to Perdition,* she has earned a reputation for perfectionism. In 1981, shortly after leaving Stagedoor Manor, she played an anorexic in the TV movie *The Best Little Girl in the World,* starving herself down to a frightening weight of eighty-six pounds. No one who met Jennifer Jason Leigh (née Jenny Morrow) at Stagedoor Manor in the summer of 1977 would have been surprised by this display of determination. At a young age, her work ethic was already well established. That summer she'd starred as Laura Wingfield, the physically and emotionally crippled center of *The Glass Menagerie.* "You'd see her limping into the cafeteria," says Todd Graff. "She was already into Method acting then."

Caitlin Van Zandt (*Guiding Light*) spent ten summers at Stagedoor. In her last, she starred in Sondheim's *Assassins* playing Sara Jane Moore, the former nursing student who attempted to assassinate President Gerald Ford in 1975. "Sara Jane Moore did one interview— in *Playboy,*" Caitlin says. "I was desperate to read it." Her character research wouldn't be complete without it. And so (with permission from Stagedoor) she logged on to a computer in the main office and bought that issue of *Playboy* off eBay. "There I am at Stagedoor," she says, "reading a vintage 1976 *Playboy* for research."

Jon Cryer (CBS's *Two And a Half Men*) is flanked by Jack Romano (left) and Carl Samuelson at an early Stagedoor Manor awards ceremony.

"Everyone at camp was always losing their voices," says Amy B. Harris, a writer for *Sex and the City*. "And so, one summer, everyone sucked on garlic. Garlic! Someone said that garlic helped clear sore throats or laryngitis. So we asked the kitchen to order it for us. We were sucking on garlic 24/7. It was disgusting."

Yancey Arias, who played Thuy in Broadway's *Miss Saigon* (and more recently starred in NBC's reboot of *Knight Rider*), was in a production of *The Me Nobody Knows* at Stagedoor in the late '80s. He had one line—and in the dress rehearsal for the show, he flubbed it. "You will never make it if you can't remember one fucking line!" Jack Romano shouted. Yancey, who was already auditioning regularly in New York, was so embarrassed, so disappointed in himself, that he considered giving it all up right then. He ran outside the Playhouse. "I looked up to the sky in tears," Yancey says. *"Give me a sign! Am I supposed to be an actor?"* At that moment, a star shot across the sky. Yancey rubbed his eyes and demanded another sign. "Five seconds later," Yancey says. "another shooting star. And I never questioned it again. I went running around camp shouting my one line."

Shawn Levy, whose film *Night at the Museum: Battle of the Smithsonian* made $177 million dollars at the U.S. box office while I was researching this book, recalls his first show at Stagedoor. "I was Danny Zuko in *Grease* at thirteen years old! First show! First audition! Lead role! I could win an Academy Award and I wouldn't have the pride I still feel over playing Danny Zuko. I sang 'Corner of the Sky' from *Pippin* in the Our Time Cabaret. *I owned that shit.* To this day, I will on occasion sing 'Corner of the Sky' for my daughters. I'm too ashamed to belt it out in front of my wife, but I'll let it rip for my girls. I wasn't blessed with sons. I won't know the joy of playing catch in my backyard. But running lines and singing harmony with my daughters is a close second." It's not hyperbole. Shawn Levy bought a summer home not far from Stagedoor, and in 2009 he stopped in at camp see a show. When he touched Jack Romano's photograph hanging in the Playhouse, he broke down in tears.

He wasn't alone. That same weekend, the actor Sebastian Stan (a Stagedoor alum) returned to camp with his girlfriend, *Gossip Girl*'s Leighton Meester. "Sebastian warned me that he might get emotional," Leighton says. "And at that cabaret thing, he and his friend were crying. So I started crying, too."

Being a Stagedoor person? As opposed to someone who just passed through Loch Sheldrake? Perhaps it starts with appreciating these anecdotes. Because the commitment to suck on garlic (for the good of the show), to limp into the cafeteria (for the character!), to rely on celestial intervention—this passion for the craft and zeal for performance is what Stagedoor people live for. Why do anything in life if you won't commit completely? Where's the excitement if there are no stakes?

But going on to a successful professional career in the arts isn't a prerequisite for being a Stagedoor person. Sometimes, maybe *helping* a Stagedoor person is enough. Ally Hilfiger, Tommy Hilfiger's daughter, appeared as an old woman in a Stagedoor production of Bertolt Brecht's *The Good Person of Szechwan*. She strains to remember the details of the show. What she *does* remember is an incredible young actor from England whom she'd met that summer. "He was really passionate about the play *Death of a Salesman*," Ally Hilfiger recalls. "But he was poor! I heard he was coming to New York after that summer. *Death of a Salesman* was playing on Broadway. And so I bought him tickets—and sent them to him anonymously."

When I spoke with Stagedoor alumni, there was a concern that the culture of the camp had somehow changed: the idea that Stagedoor must now be populated by robot kids bent on fame. That being a Stagedoor person was becoming synonymous with having the drive, talent, and determination to *make it*. And there was some of that. Natalie Walker, one of the most talented kids in 2009, expressed similar concerns. "When you get leads at Stagedoor Manor," she says, "it can start the wheels spinning."

There's a fear among parents and alumni that having high expectations creates bitterness and disappointment later in life, that the camp encourages kids to set unrealistic goals. "There are a lot of damaged people out there, damaged for being so emotionally involved for three weeks at Stagedoor Manor," says Keith Levenson (who has conducted the New York Philharmonic). "The people who wanted to be in show business but who aren't and are bitter about it—they'll be harder for you to find. But there are probably many, many more of those out there. Fifteen percent of these kids would have been stars anyway. Eighty-five percent were lost kids, and their parents were just paying for them to be in a show."

But after my three weeks at Stagedoor, I couldn't help but ask: What would be so wrong with that? I'd come to realize that being a Stagedoor Manor person has nothing to do with talent and everything to do with heart. Theater people tend to be superstitious, not religious, but I'll risk quoting scripture to make a point. Psalm 68: "God sets the lonely in families, he leads forth the prisoners with singing."

"Most of these kids have never been, and never will be, involved in theater in a remotely professional way," says Eric Nightengale, founder of Manhattan's 78th Street Theater Lab, who directed at Stagedoor for four summers. "That doesn't matter here any more than it matters at a soccer camp. What matters is the expectations set by the peer group, where they find themselves in an environment being asked to do something they have secretly loved and have had to hide from their friends at home. Whether or not you attain the dream of Broadway doesn't matter. Just beginning to *entertain* that kind of dream is transformational."

Supremely talented or just enthusiastic about theater, these kids at Stagedoor Manor—like the kids at Beginners Showcase in Georges Mills, New Hampshire, forty years earlier, like me sitting in the orchestra of a Broadway show crying at the overture—wanted a second home where they could be accepted and loved for who they are. The Stagedoor Mafia? The so-called job network? Sure, it exists—to a point. The name alone won't get you in the room, but it might help you stay in the room for a few extra minutes. What $5,000 in tuition gets you is a family and a support network. No matter how easy it is now to connect with other theater geeks on the Web, nothing could ever replace the feeling of a teacher really seeing you for the first time.

"Stagedoor provided a home for wayward kids," says Jeanine Tesori. "Jack Romano provided a foundation for people, including me, who were floundering a bit and at a big crossroads in their lives."

In early September 2009, Stagedoor Manor received word that the organizers of the Macy's Thanksgiving Day Parade wanted to include the camp in that year's festivities. They would install the Stagedoor kids on the final float alongside Santa Claus himself, where they'd perform a Christmas song written specifically for the occasion. Panic set in. Stagedoor campers, now back at home enmeshed in the new school year, were suddenly begging their parents to change long-planned Thanksgiving vacations, just for the *chance* to be considered for the parade. No one was more excited than Cindy Samuelson. "My mother loved the parade," she says. "We always watched. She passed away on Thanksgiving. This will be really special for me."

The Macy's Thanksgiving Day Parade? Was this exactly the kind of event to make skeptical alums wonder if the place was selling out? It's not as if the Samuelsons aren't aware of the contradictions. "The biggest challenge the camp faces," says Jonathan Samen, Cindy's husband and partner in the camp, "is to be true to its mission. To continue to be that place that so many kids want and need to feel safe."

When it came to careerism, it would be foolish to think one could possibly put the worms back in the can. The talent scouts from Disney, the world premiere productions—that sure is a nice talking point, but it would never be more than just that. The heart of the summer camp experience, as an institution, has been, and always will be, about expanding minds in a safe environment. That's the camp's struggle. To remain a safe space for kids to be kids, which is to say, for kids to make mistakes. That is what this generation is in danger of losing.

Sometimes it takes a child to remind you where the emphasis should be.

There is a staff talent show every session at Stagedoor Manor. In 2009, Erich Rausch, the music director for *West Side Story* comes out onstage to deliver a monologue. At age forty, he's returning to acting in his own life, and he took the opportunity tonight to perform a monologue about impending marriage. To set the scene, he enlists a female counselor to stand behind him in a veil. The first minute goes off without incident. But then Erich begins to flub his lines. He breaks out into a cold sweat. He reaches into his pocket for the script. Unfortunately, his cheat sheet has ripped at the seams. He is trying to piece the scraps back together on stage, in front of three hundred campers. He starts muttering to himself, "Man, I really don't know this piece." It is horribly uncomfortable. And the older kids start snickering.

And then, just when it appears Erich might exit the stage and write the whole thing off as an unfortunate mistake, a word of encouragement comes from the most unlikely source: a ten-year-old girl seated cross-legged directly in front of the stage who shouts, "It's okay. It's Stagedoor!"

Erich proudly finishes the monologue.

———

Rachael Singer left Stagedoor Manor for the last time on Sunday morning. Eating lunch with her family at Newark Airport shortly before takeoff, she broke down in tears. She was that sick, but also heartbroken. She barely got out of bed at home over the next week, and was still feeling run-down a week later, while on vacation with her parents and siblings to celebrate her graduation from high school and to enjoy each other's company before this next stage of their lives begins. Finally, Rachael had time to reflect on *Sweeney Todd*—both the journey itself, and the time in the infirmary that threatened to hijack the hard-earned progress she'd made. "I didn't think I could pull it off," she says. "It wasn't a typical Rachael role. It wasn't tap-dancing. It wasn't bubbly. I could have used more time to grow into the character. But I did a pretty good job, I think. I let my guard down. I wasn't afraid to go for it." She thought for a moment. "You can do more than your stereotypical role." She was packing for The Boston Conservatory when we spoke last, nervous about what she'd find there. "There will be so many talented people. I'll have to work hard. And that's what I want. I want that push."

Harry Katzman returned home to South Carolina. It was a tough summer. He largely retreated from his social life, preferring to spend time with just a few close friends. He was preemptively severing ties— a scary thought, but also perhaps freeing. He'd survived adolescence, which is all one can reasonably hope for.

His mother and stepfather planned to drop Harry off at the University of Michigan in September. He was hoping they'd get to speak with Brent Wagner, the head of the school's prestigious theater department. Harry worries that his parents think that, by majoring in theater, he's somehow majoring in being Harry. "They won't realize what I'm getting myself into until they hear it from Wagner," Harry says.

For now, in Columbia, South Carolina, the toilets await. Harry got a summer job working for what he thought was a restaurant and catering company. He figured he'd make seven dollars an hour as a busboy. But it turns out he's working as the owner's lackey. This woman operates a cleaning business, too, and when Harry reports to work on some days, she sends him out with the cleaning crew. "I'm scrubbing toilets and floors," Harry says. "Glamorous!" His boss supplements her staff with a handful of Hispanic workers, and sometimes Harry has to borrow his mother's car to pick up this cleaning crew. One afternoon, he sits in the car with a young Mexican woman. "It was so awkward," Harry says. "We couldn't really communicate. I don't speak Spanish. She looked terrified. But I wanted her to feel at home."

What's a theater geek to do? "I put on the CD of *In the Heights*," Harry says, referring to the Latino-flavored Broadway musical about Dominican-Americans in Washington Heights. "It was the most silent car ride ever."

Brian Muller, meanwhile, was due at rehearsals for *Little House on the Prairie*. He'd been cast as the wily student Clarence, a troublemaker in Laura Ingalls's classroom, and the forty-one-week, twenty-six-city national tour would kick off in September at the famed Paper Mill Playhouse in New Jersey. At rehearsal on the first day, a rep from Actors' Equity spoke for an hour about joining the union, about health insurance and retirement plans. "I don't think I have dental," Brian says, smirking at the rush of adulthood, the absurdity of his being able to make such a statement just weeks after leaving summer camp. He was rehearsing on the third floor of a well-known Broadway studio space at 229 West 42nd Street. Luckily, he had help in easing this otherwise jarring transition. His good friend Noah Robbins, another one-time Stagedoor camper, was on the ninth floor preparing to make his Broadway debut in *Brighton Beach Memoirs*.

For his part, Brian impressed the *Prairie* director early on. "Theater camp can teach you craft," says Francesca Zambello, who respects Brian for his obvious talent, his good manners (her words), and the thoughtfulness he brings to rehearsal. "But you need that It factor. And Brian has it."

In September 2009, more than fifteen of Brian's friends from Stagedoor take the train to the Paper Mill to see him open the show. "We're here to see Clarence," one jokes to the usher, unamused, who scans his ticket without looking up. They take their seats in the balcony, sticking out among the many young families in the audience tonight.

And the show begins. Brian comes out in the first number, looking like a pioneer, carrying a leather shoulder bag and a pickax, singing about the thrill of the American frontier and the great move westward. But his featured moment comes in act two, when he tortures Laura Ingalls in her one-room schoolhouse. Clarence is the disruptive student, and Brian scoots around the stage, teasing his younger classmates, stealing one's hat, and generally making a scene. Meanwhile, the Stagedoor campers are doing the same upstairs. Every time Brian opens his mouth, one can hear outsized laughs of approval wafting down from his cheering section.

Backstage, a cast member says to Brian, "So, I guess your friends are here tonight?"

Acknowledgments

Thank you to Wylie O'Sullivan, Sharbari Bose Kamat, Sydney Tanigawa, Farley Chase, Howard Sanders, Jim Nelson, Michael Hainey, Mark Kirby, Thomas Alberty, Jason Gay, Mark Healy, Joshua Jacobson, Danielle Nussbaum, Marshall Heyman, Seth Fradkoff, Nicole Vecchiarelli, Jon Kelly, Rebecca Sinn, Siddhartha Lokanandi, Dominick Amista, Dominick and Maria DeNicolo, Dave Itzkoff, Cindy Samuelson, Debra Samuelson, Jonathan Samen, Konnie Kittrell, David Quinn, Mark Saks, Michael Larsen, Alexandra Shiva, Jonathan Marc Sherman, Amy Brownstein, Stephen Agosto, Marcus Baker, Bradford Carter, Travis Greisler, Justin Mendoza, Raymond Zilberberg, Corin "Pinky" Miller, Peter Green, Jeffrey Zeiner, Andrea Oliveri, Brian Bumbery, Elizabeth Spiridakis, and the many alumni of Beginners Showcase and Stagedoor Manor who graciously shared their stories with me. A special thanks to the late Kate Sullivan—the closest thing I had to a Jack Romano—and to Julio Gambuto, Jon and Erin Rapkin, and my parents, Jane and Lenny Rapkin.

Index

About the Author

Mickey Rapkin is a senior editor at *GQ* magazine. His first book, *Pitch Perfect: The Quest for Collegiate A Cappella Glory,* was published by Gotham Books in 2008. Rapkin has written for the *New York Times* and *Entertainment Weekly.* He lives in Manhattan.